MW00785313

Scott Foresman

Reading

Grade 1

Phonics Workbook

Scott Foresman Phonics System™

Scott Foresman

Editorial Offices: Glenview, Illinois • New York, New York
Sales Offices: Reading, Massachusetts • Duluth, Georgia • Glenview, Illinois
Carrollton, Texas • Menlo Park, California

Skill	Page Numbers

Skill	Page Numbers

Name ______________________________

Draw lines.

1.	V	2.	I
A		H	
	A		H
3.	B	4.	M
D		M	
	D		N
5.	Z	6.	D
S		B	
	S		B
7.	C	8.	W
G		W	
	G		V

Directions: Draw lines to match the letters.

Home Activity: Show a page of a book and have your child point to letters that look alike.

Name ______________________________

Circle.

1.	E	E	L	E	F
2.	V	W	V	V	U
3.	L	T	I	L	L
4.	Z	Z	K	H	Z
5.	P	B	P	R	P

Directions: In each row, circle the letters that are the same as the first letter.

Home Activity: Write the alphabet on paper and have your child name letters as you point to them.

Name ____________________

Draw lines.

1.	o	2.	f
c		f	
	c		t
3.	i	4.	m
i		n	
	j		n
5.	n	6.	k
r		k	
	r		h
7.	y	8.	j
q		y	
	q		y

Directions: Draw lines to match the letters.

Home Activity: Point to a letter on the page and ask your child to name the letter.

Name ______________________________

Circle.

1.	o	e	o	c	o
2.	g	p	g	g	y
3.	x	w	x	v	x
4.	l	l	t	l	i
5.	h	n	h	r	h

Directions: In each row, circle the letters that are the same as the first letter.

Home Activity: Have your child choose a letter and write the letter on a sheet of paper.

Name ______________________________

Draw lines.

1. A — a, c
2. S — Z, s
3. W — w, v
4. E — c, e
5. R — n, r
6. C — c, o
7. L — t, l
8. Q — q, g

Directions: Draw lines to match the letters.

Home Activity: Use letter cards and have your child match the capital and lowercase letters.

Name ______________________

m 

Write.

1. 

2. 

3. 

4. 

5. 

6. 

7. 

8. 

9. 

10. 

11. 

12. 

Directions: Write the letter *m* if the picture name begins like *monkey.*

Home Activity: Look through magazines and books for pictures of things that begin with *m.*

Name ______________________

r 

Write.

1. ______ 

2. ______ 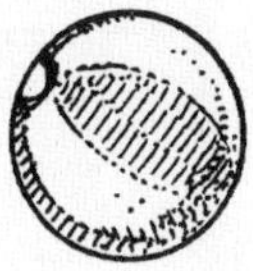

3. ______ 

4. ______ 

5. ______ 

6. ______ 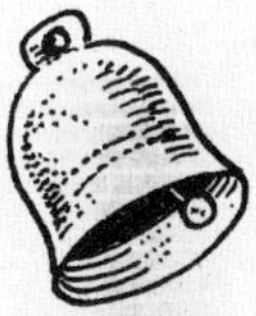

7. ______ 

8. ______ 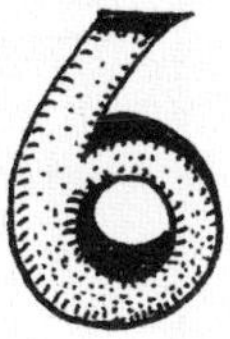

9. ______ 

10. ______ 

11. ______ 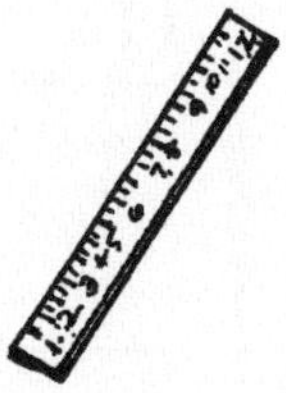

12. ______ 

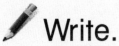

Directions: Write the letter *r* if the picture name begins like *rabbit.*

Home Activity: Say a word. If the word begins like *rabbit,* have your child point to the rabbit at the top of the page.

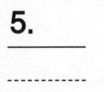

Name ______________________

s

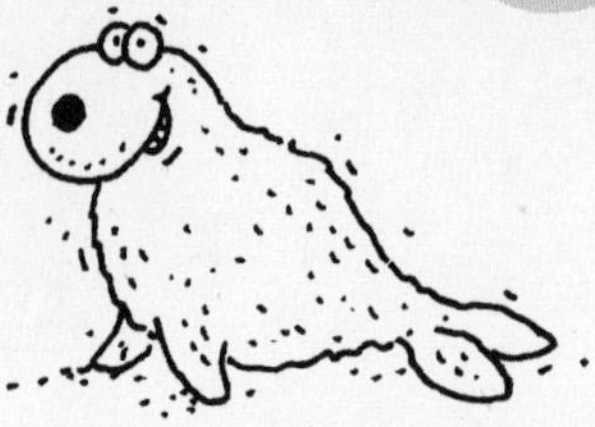

Write.

1. 

2. 

3. 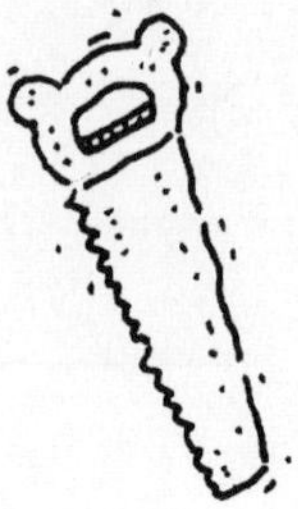

4. 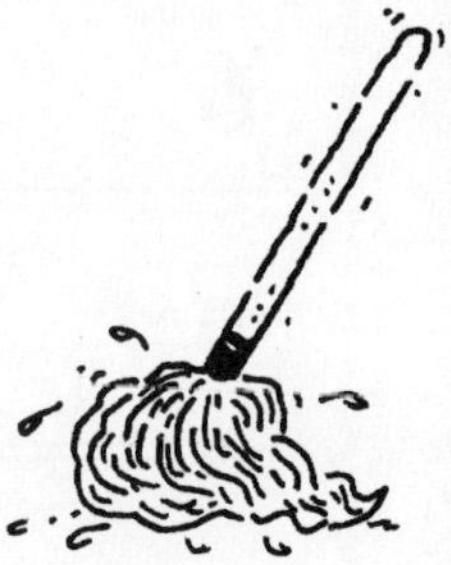

5. 

6. 

7. 

8. 

9. 

10. 

11. 

12. 

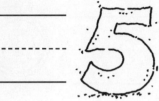

Directions: Write the letter *s* if the picture name begins like *seal.*

Home Activity: Say two words and ask your child to tell which word begins like *seal.*

Name ____________________

b 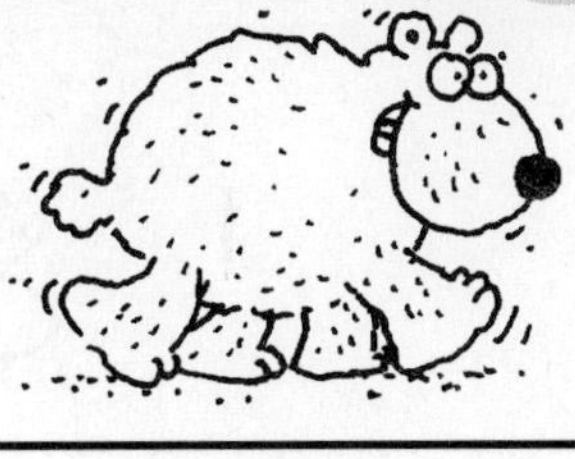

Write.

1. 

2. 

3. 

4. 

5. 

6. 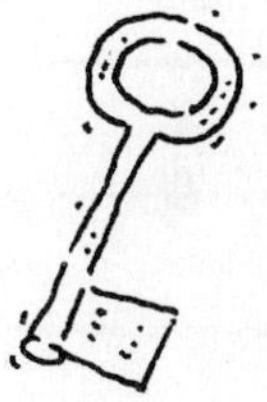

7. 

8. 

9. 

10. 

11. 

12. 

Directions: Write the letter *b* if the picture name begins like *bear.*

Home Activity: Point to an object in the room and ask your child to name a word that begins with the same sound.

Name ______________________

t 

Write.

1.

2.
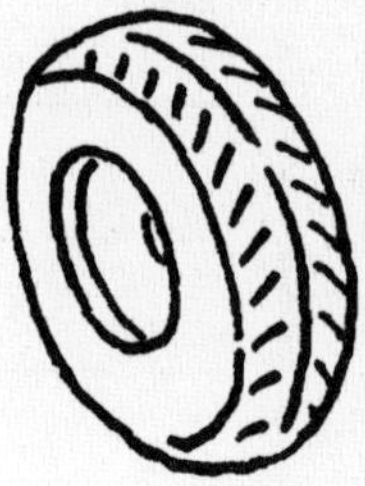

3.

4.

5.

6.

7.

8.

9.

10.

11.

12.
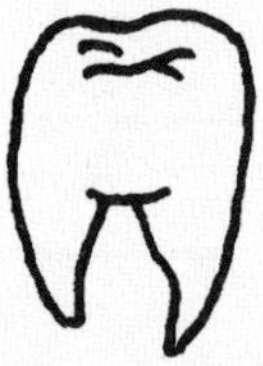

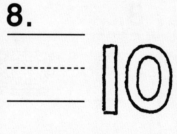

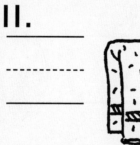

Directions: Write the letter *t* if the picture name begins like *turtle.*

Home Activity: Write several letter *t*'s on paper and ask your child to name a word that begins with *t* and circle a letter.

Name ______________________

c 

Write.

1. 

2. 

3. 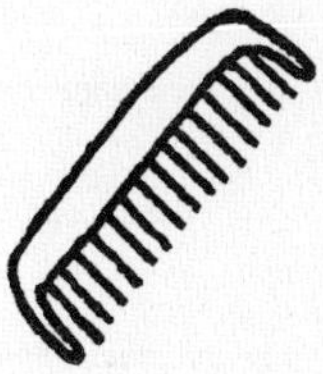

4. 

5. 

6. 

7. 

8. 

9. 

10. 

11. 

12. 

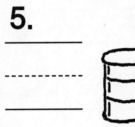

Directions: Write the letter *c* if the picture name begins like *cat.*

Home Activity: Say a picture name and have your child point to the picture and name the letter for the beginning sound.

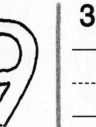

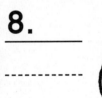

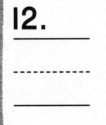

n 

Write.

1. 

2. 

3. 

4. 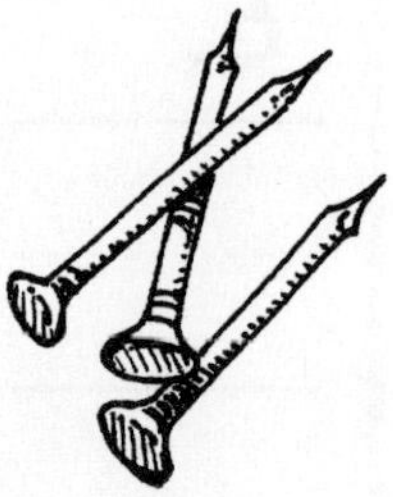

5. 

6. 

7. 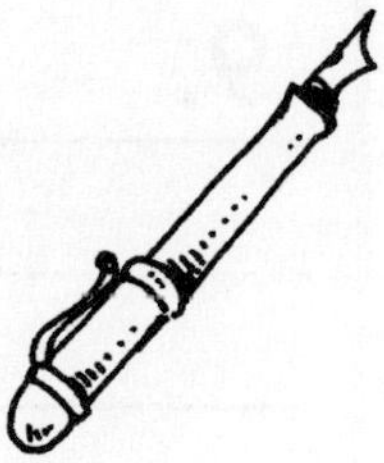

8. 

9. 

10. 

11. 

12. 

Directions: Write the letter *n* if the picture name begins like *nest.*

Home Activity: Give a clue to an *n* word and have your child name the word—*holds up your head, used for smelling.*

p 

Write.

1. 

2. 

3. 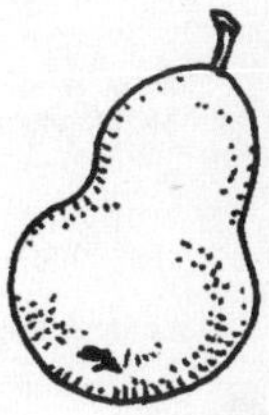

4. 

5. 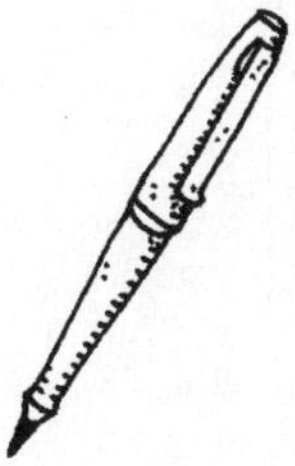

6. 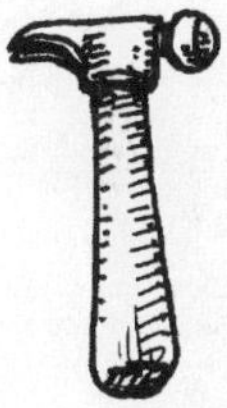

7. 

8. 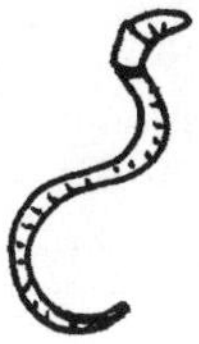

9. 

10. 

11. 

12. 

Directions: Write the letter *p* if the picture name begins like *pig*.

Home Activity: Hold up a pencil and ask your child to name words that begin like *pencil*.

Name ______________________

Circle.

1.

can

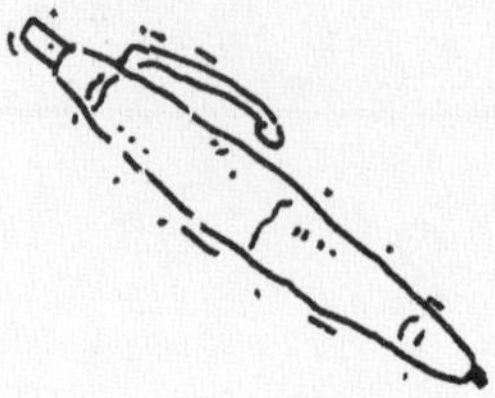

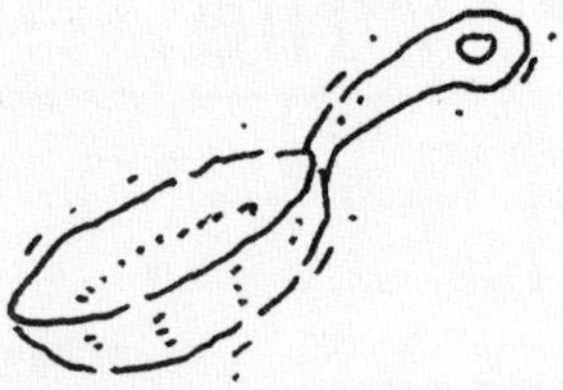

2.

cat

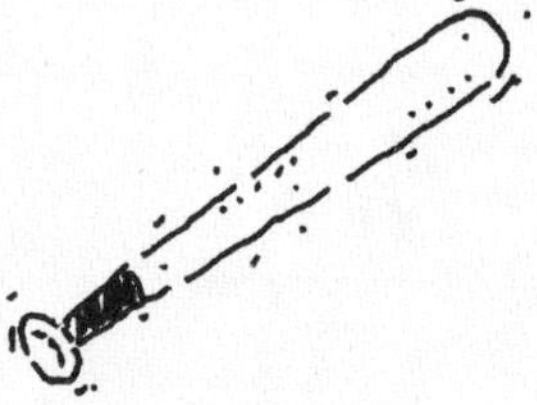

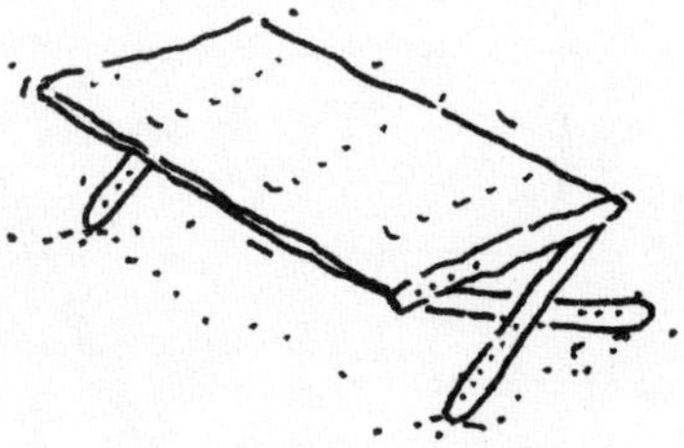

3.

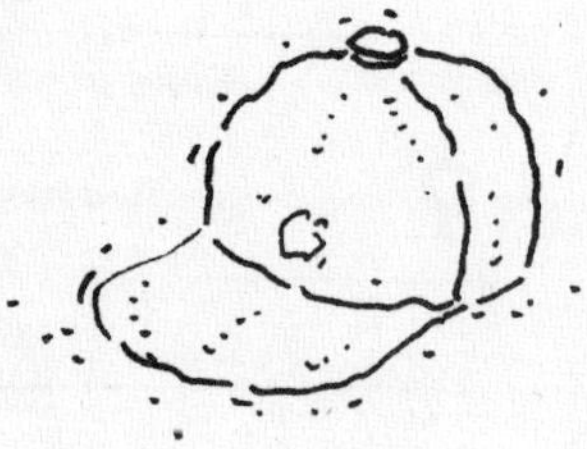

cap

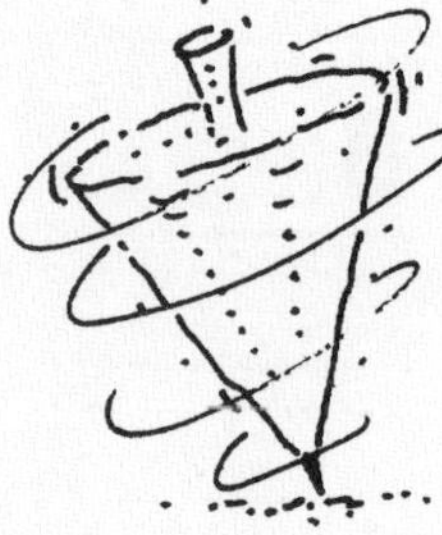

4.

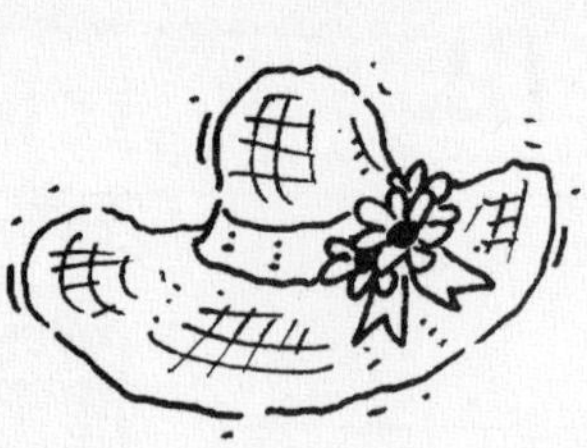

hat

Directions: In each row, circle the picture whose name rhymes with the first word.

Home Activity: Help your child name other rhyming words for the words on the page.

Name ______________________________

Write.

1.  

cat

____

2. 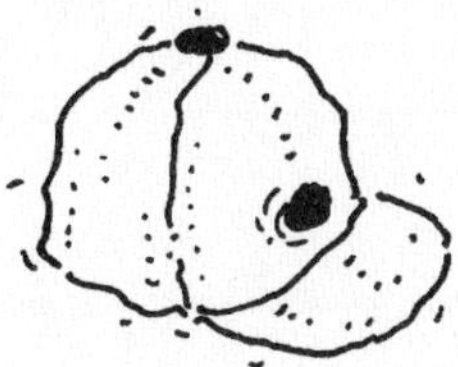 

cap

____

3. 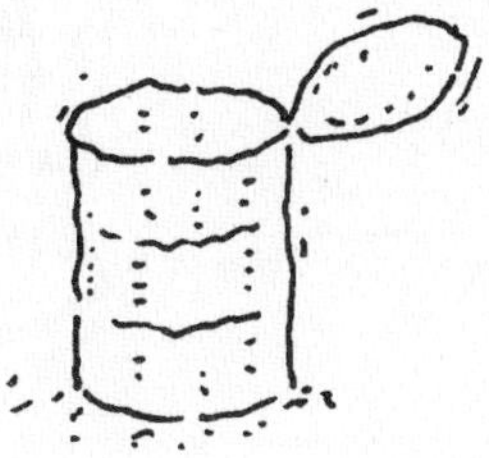 

can

____

4. 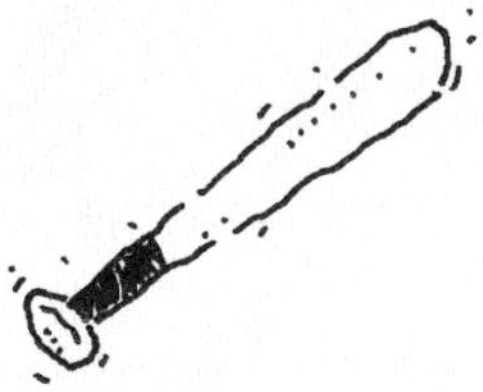 

bat

____

5.  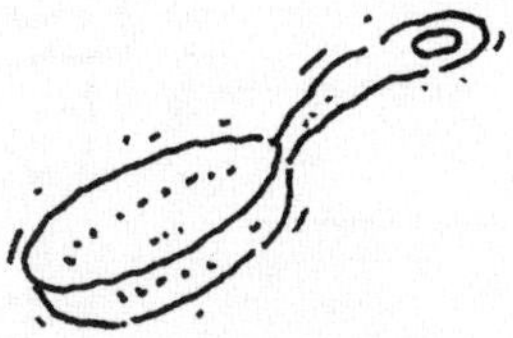

man

____

Directions: Write the rhyming word that names the picture.

Home Activity: Ask your child to use the rhyming words in a sentence.

Name ______________________________

f 

Write.

1. 

2. 

3. 

4. 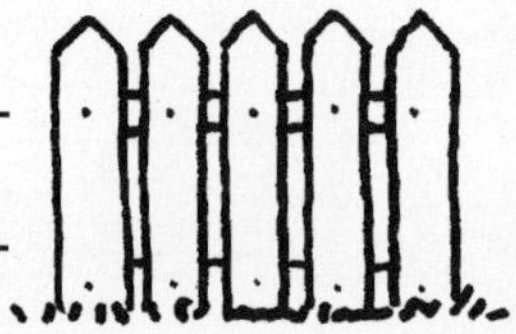

5. 

6. 

7. 

8. 

9. 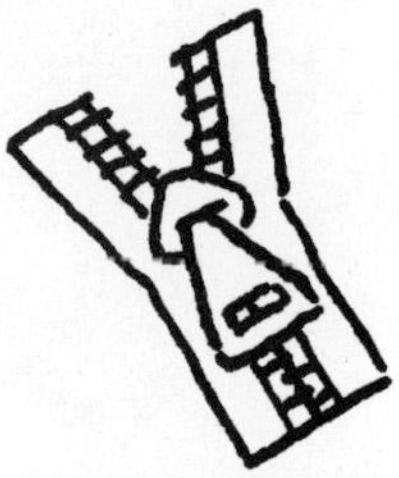

10. 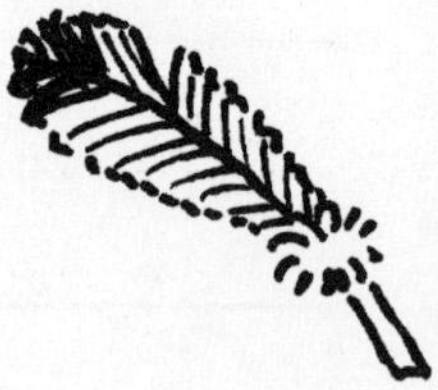

11. 

12. 

Directions: Write the letter *f* if the picture name begins like *fish*.

Home Activity: Say a word from the page and have your child hold up four fingers if the word begins like *four fingers*.

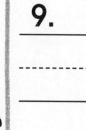

Name ______________________________

g 

Write.

1. 

2. 

3. 

4. 

5. 

6. 

7. 

8. 

9. 

10. 

11. 

12. 

Directions: Write the letter *g* if the picture name begins like *goat*.

Home Activity: Help your child create phrases with *g* words: *Gus's good guitar, Gabby's garden gate.*

Name ______________________

l 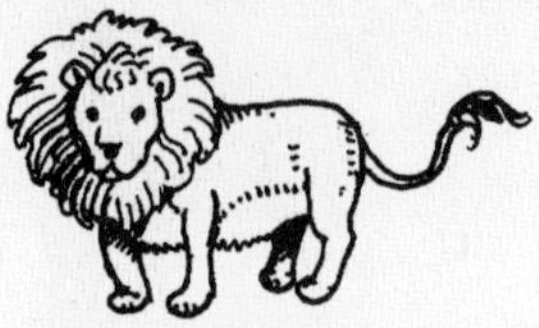

Write.

1. ____ 

2. ____ 

3. ____ 

4. ____ 

5. ____ 

6. ____ 

7. ____ 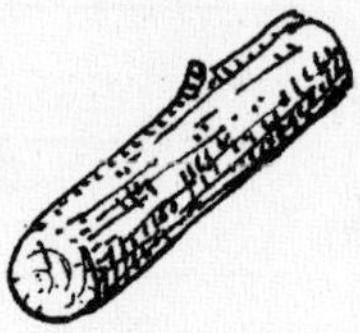

8. ____ 

9. ____ 

10. ____ 

11. ____ 

12. ____ 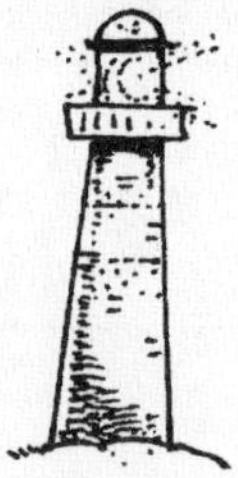

Directions: Write the letter *l* if the picture name begins like *lion.*

Home Activity: Point to a light in your home and have your child name words that begin like *light.*

Name ______________________________

Circle.

1.

hit

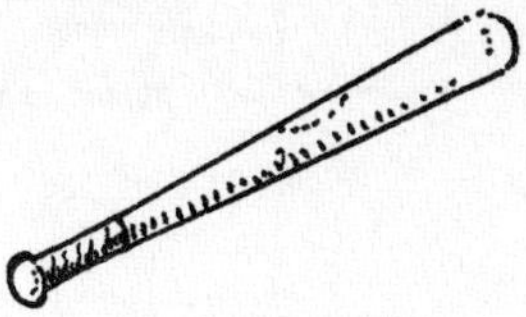

2.

dig

3.

sit

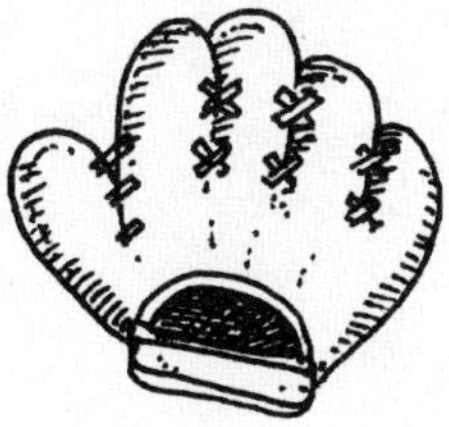

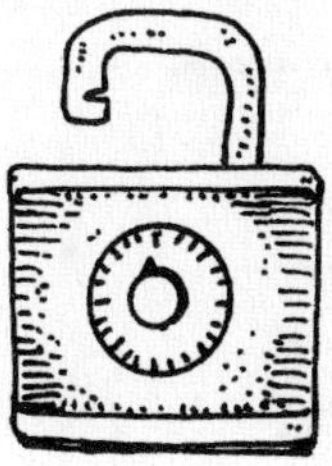

4.

big

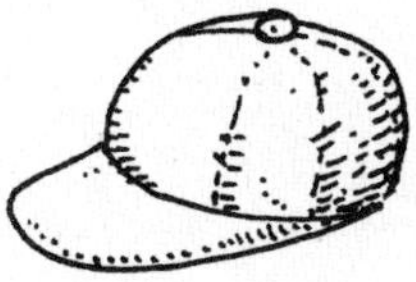

Directions: In each row, circle the picture whose name rhymes with the first word.

Home Activity: Have your child say the rhyming word pairs and add other words that rhyme.

Name ________________________________

Write.

1.

fit

2.

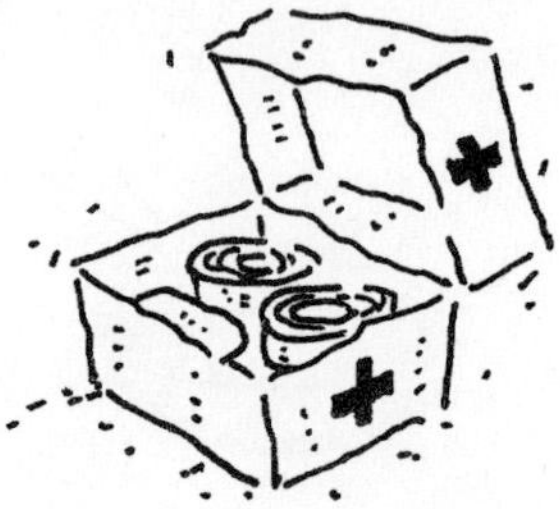

hit

3.

big

4.

fig

Directions: Write the rhyming word that names the picture.

Home Activity: Ask your child to use the rhyming words in a sentence.

Name ____________________

h 

Write.

1. 

2. 

3. 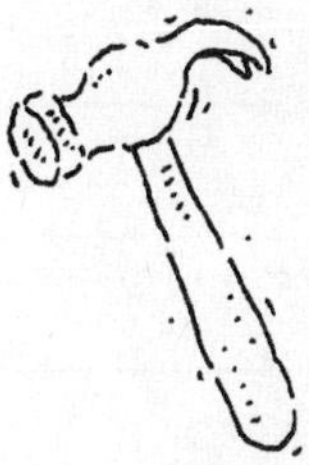

4. 

5. 

6. 

7. 

8. 

9. 

10. 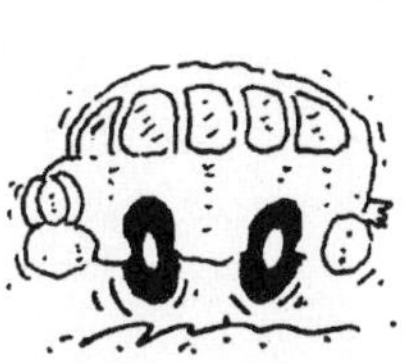

11. 

12. 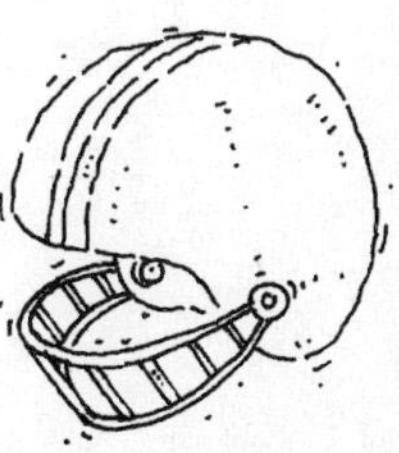

Directions: Write the letter *h* if the picture name begins like *horse.*

Home Activity: Give a riddle clue to an *h* picture and have your child give the answer: *big jungle animal, protects the head.*

Name ______________________

d

Write.

1. ________

2. ________

3. ________

4. ________

5. ________

6. ________

7. ________

8. ________

9. ________

10. ________

11. ________

12. ________

Directions: Write the letter *d* if the picture name begins like *duck.*

Home Activity: Read a story and ask your child to listen for words that begin like *duck.*

Name ______________________________

k 

Write.

1. ________ 

2. ________ 

3. ________ 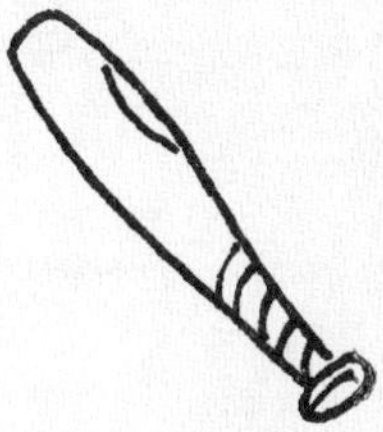

4. ________ 

5. ________ 

6. ________ 

7. ________ 

8. ________ 

9. ________ 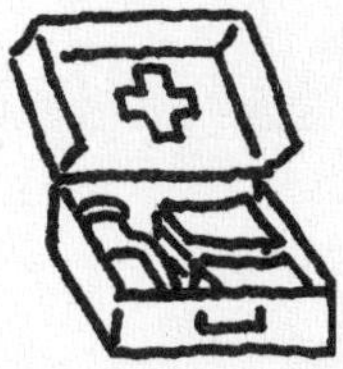

10. ________ 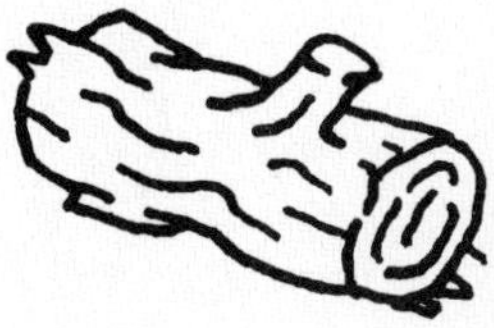

11. ________ 

12. ________ 

Directions: Write the letter *k* if the picture name begins like *kite.*

Home Activity: Draw a kite and ask your child to say words that begin with *k* and write a letter *k* on the kite for each word.

Name ____________________

Circle.

1.

hop

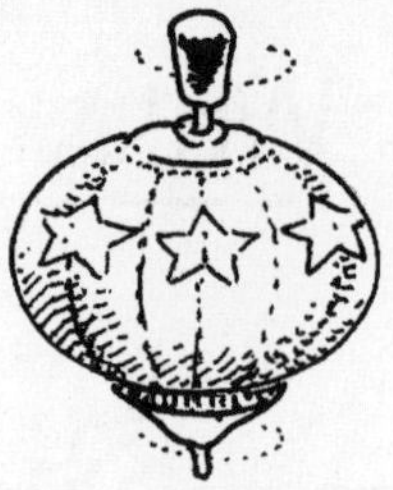

2.

mop

3.

dot

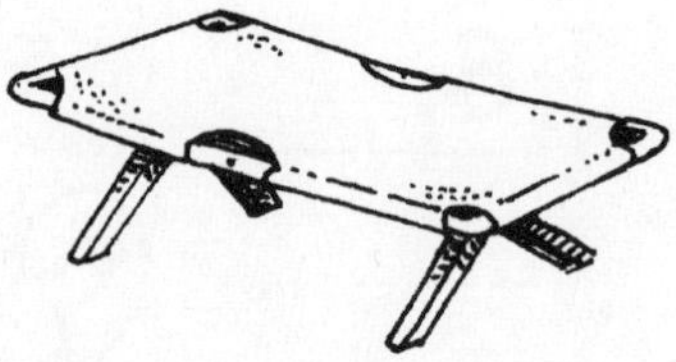

4.

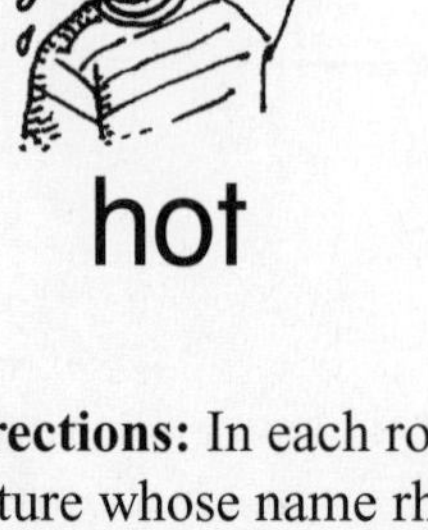

hot

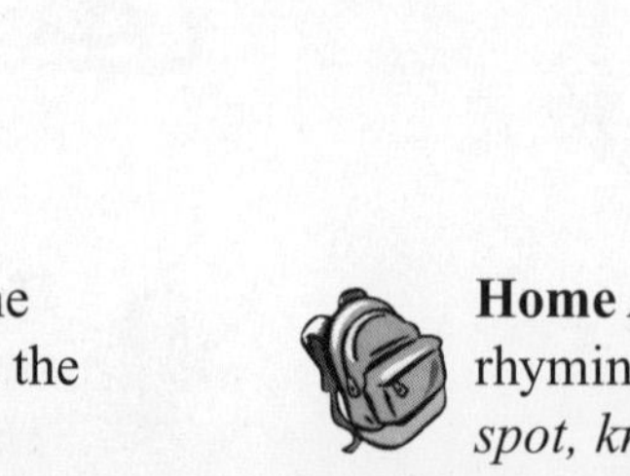

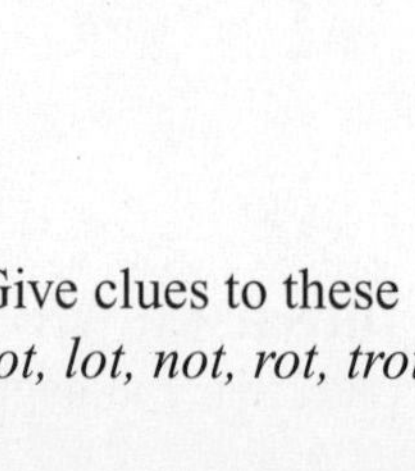

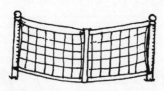

Directions: In each row, circle the picture whose name rhymes with the first word.

Home Activity: Give clues to these rhyming words: *got, lot, not, rot, trot, spot, knot.*

Name ______________________________

Write.

1.

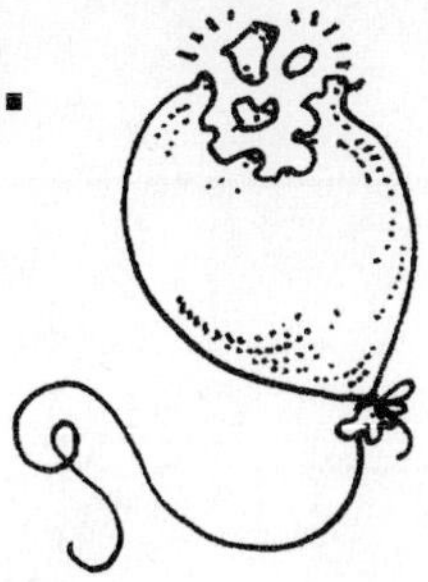

pop

2.

hop

3.

dot

4.

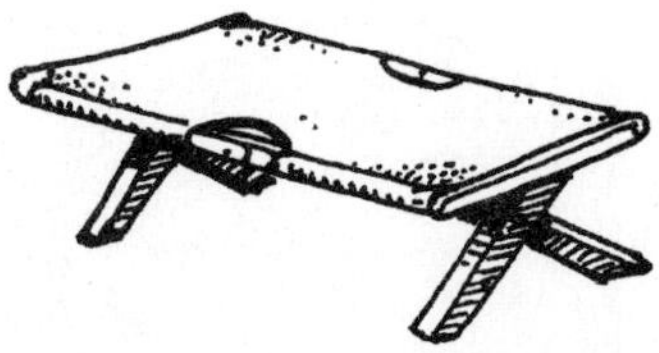

hot

Directions: Write the rhyming word that names the picture.

Home Activity: Ask your child to create a two-line rhyme: *I ran to the top. Now I can stop.*

Name ______________________

j 

Write.

1. 

2. 

3. 

4. 

5. 

6. 

7. 

8. 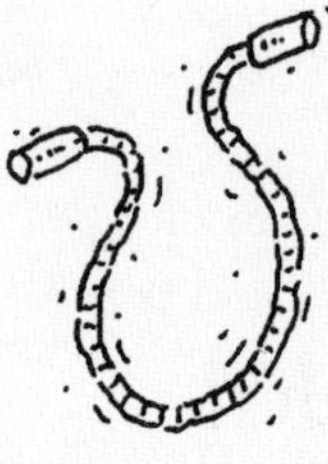

9. 

10. 

11. 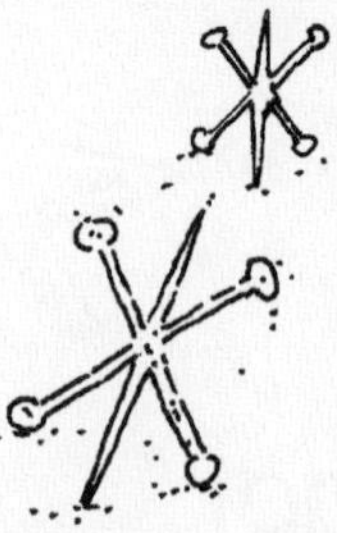

12. 

Directions: Write the letter *j* if the picture name begins like *jeep.*

Home Activity: Say words from the page and have your child jump each time a word begins like *jump.*

Name ______________________________

w 

Write.

1. 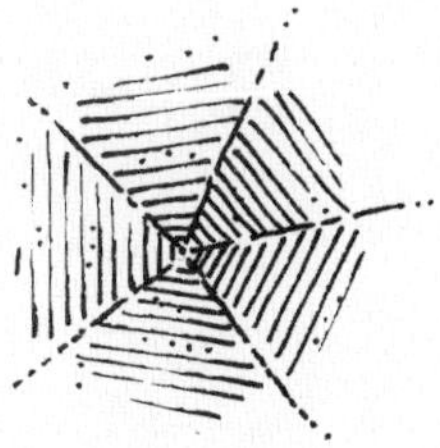

2. 

3. 

4. 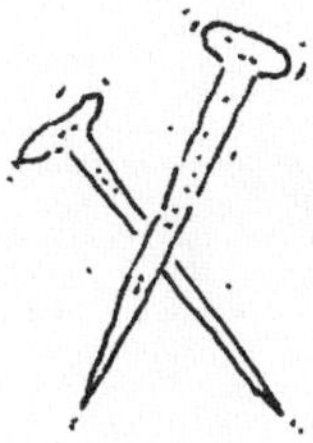

5. 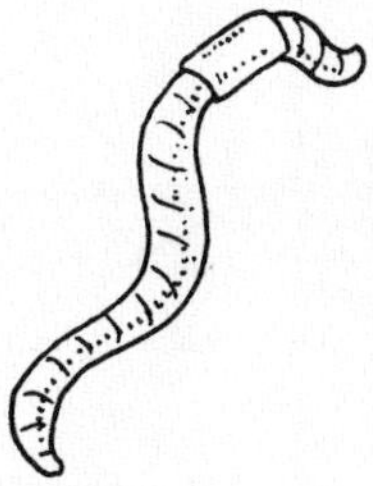

6. 

7. 

8. 

9. 

10. 

11. 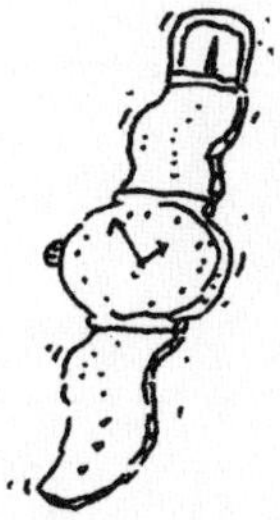

12. 

Directions: Write the letter *w* if the picture name begins like *wagon*.

Home Activity: Look through magazines and books for pictures of things that begin with *w*.

Name ______________________________

v 

Write.

1.

2.

3.

4.

5.

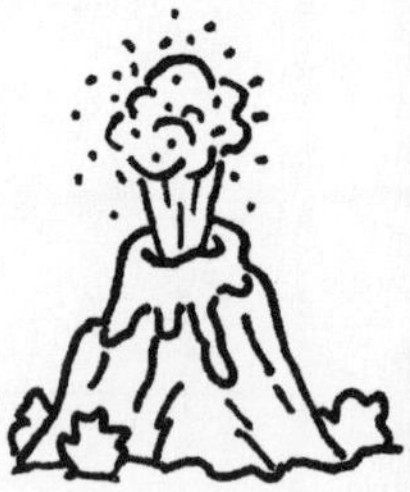

6.

7.

8.

9.

Directions: Write the letter *v* if the picture name begins like *violin.*

Home Activity: Have your child hold up two fingers to make a *v* each time you say a word that begins like *violin.*

Name ______________________________

Circle.

1.

men

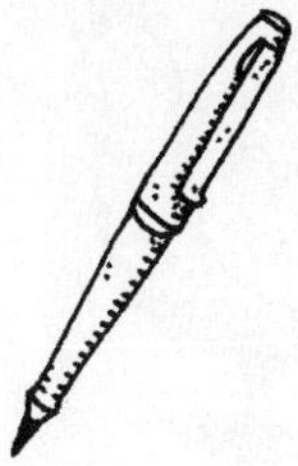

2.

hen

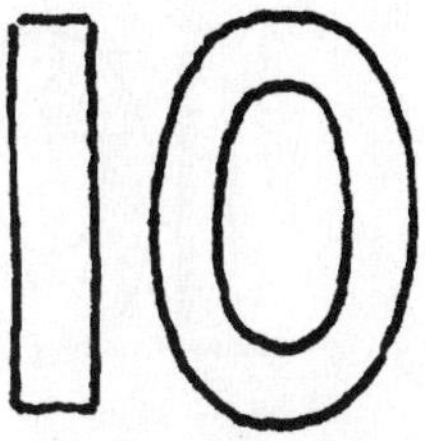

3.

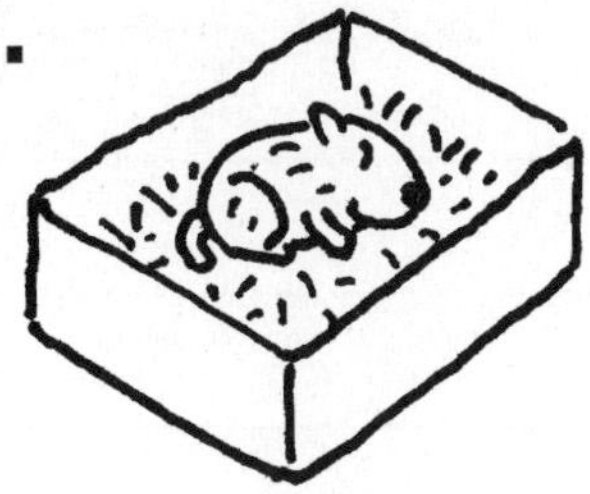

pet

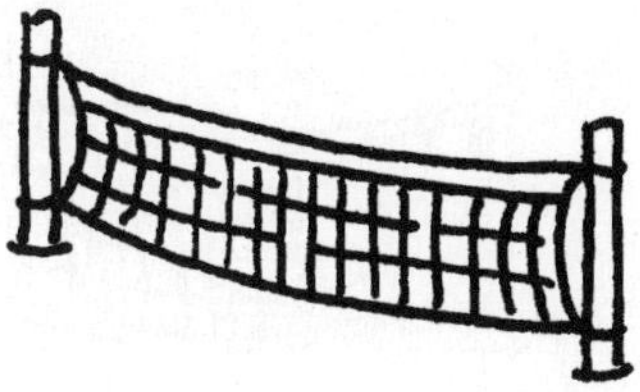

4.

vet

Directions: In each row, circle the picture whose name rhymes with the first word.

Home Activity: Have your child point to a picture and name a rhyming word.

Name ______________________

Write.

1.

hen

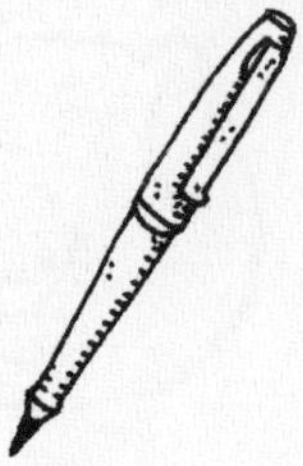

2.

men

3.

wet

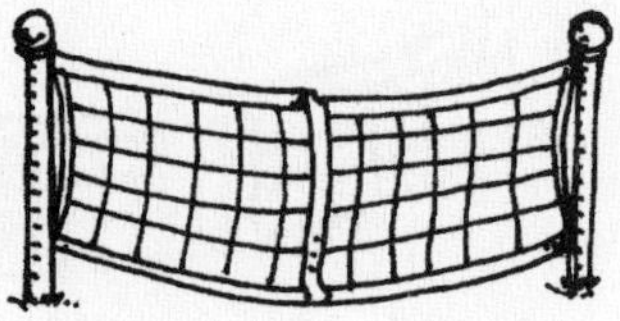

4.

pet

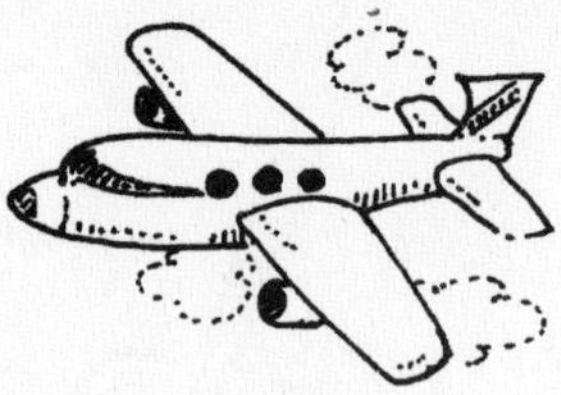

Directions: Write the rhyming word that names the picture.

Home Activity: Ask your child to use the rhyming words in a sentence.

Name ______________________

y 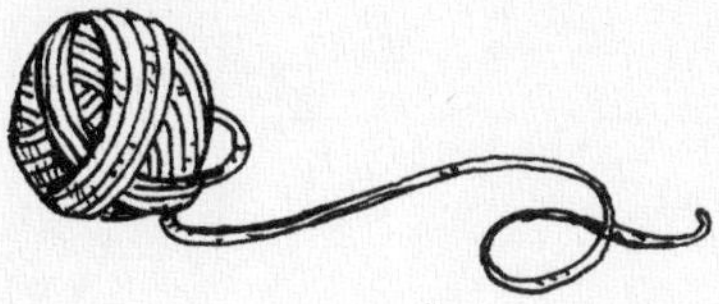

Write.

1.

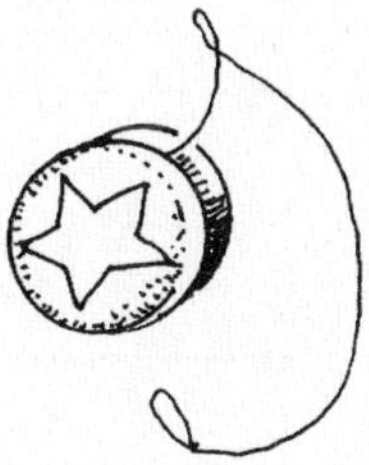

2.

3.

4.

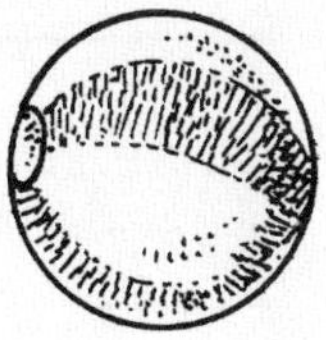

5.

6.

7.

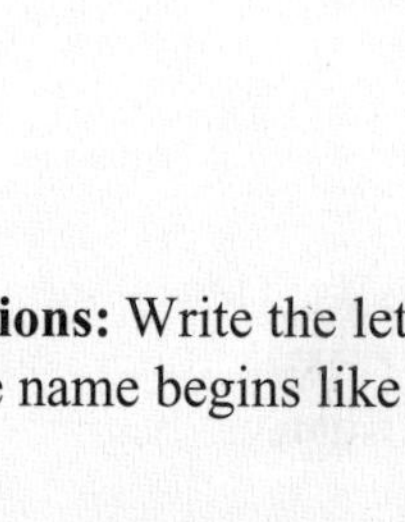

8.

9.

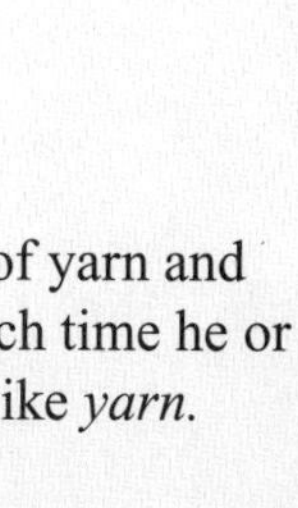

Directions: Write the letter *y* if the picture name begins like *yarn.*

Home Activity: Cut pieces of yarn and give a piece to your child each time he or she says a word that begins like *yarn.*

Name ____________________

z 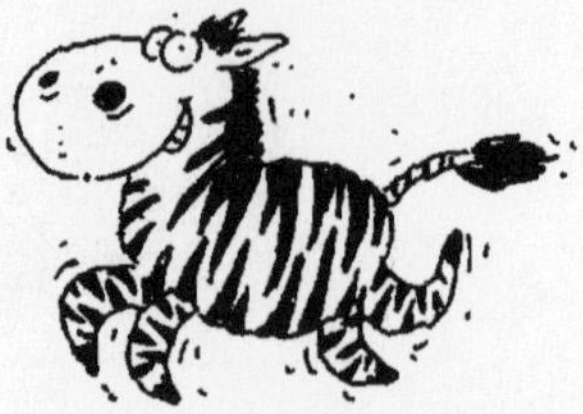

Write.

1. 

2. 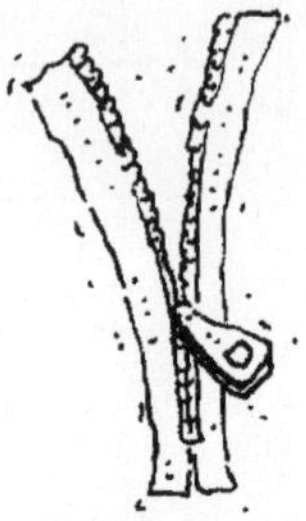

3. 

4. 

5. 

6. 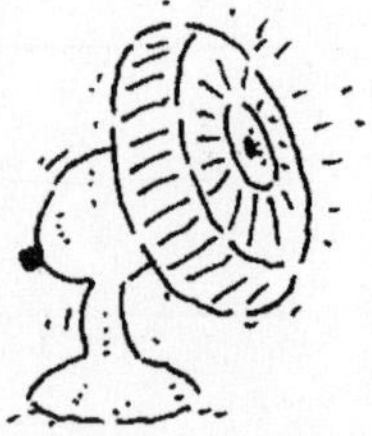

7. 

8. 

9. 

Directions: Write the letter *z* if the picture name begins like *zebra.*

Home Activity: Have your child buzz like a bee (zzzzzz) each time you point to a picture whose name begins with *z.*

x 

Write.

1. 

2. 

3. 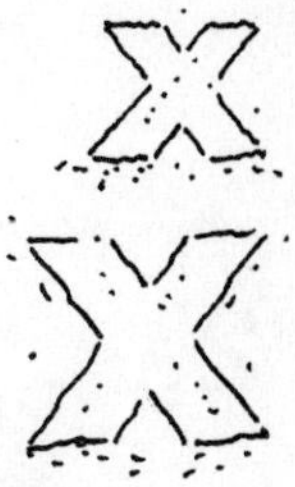

qu 

Write.

4. 

5. 

6. 

7. 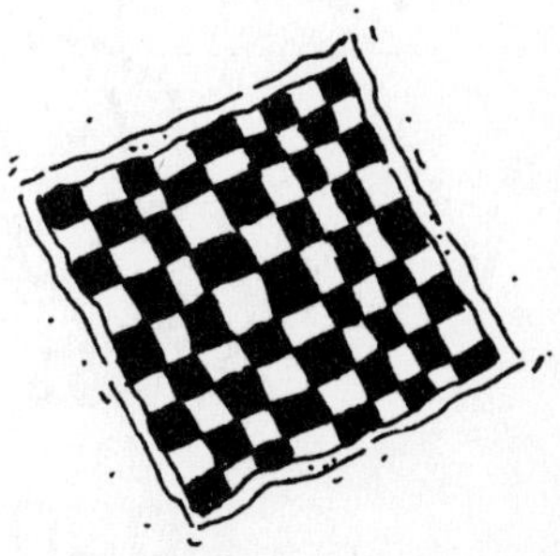

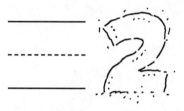

Directions: Write the letter *x* or *qu* if the picture name begins like *x ray* or *quarter.*

Home Activity: Write the letters *x* and *qu.* Have your child draw pictures of things that begin with these letters.

Name ______________________________

Circle.

1. 

bug

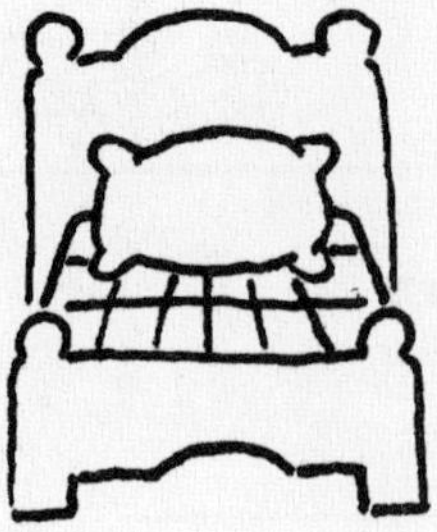 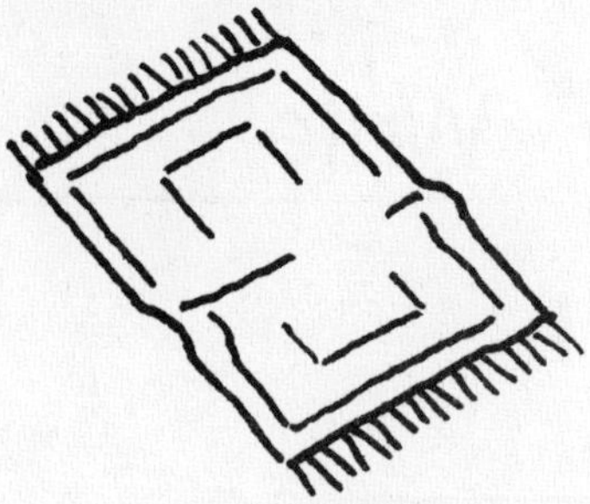

2. 

hug

3. 

cut

4. 

pup

Directions: In each row, circle the picture whose name rhymes with the first word.

Home Activity: Help your child write the rhyming picture name.

Name ____________________

Write.

1.

hug

2.

up

3.

hut

4.

dug

Directions: Write the rhyming word that names the picture.

Home Activity: Ask your child to use the rhyming words in a sentence.

Name ______________________________

cat

Color.

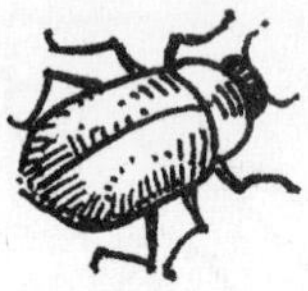

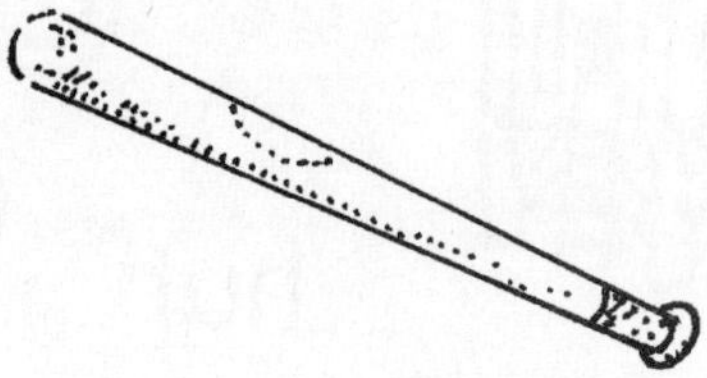

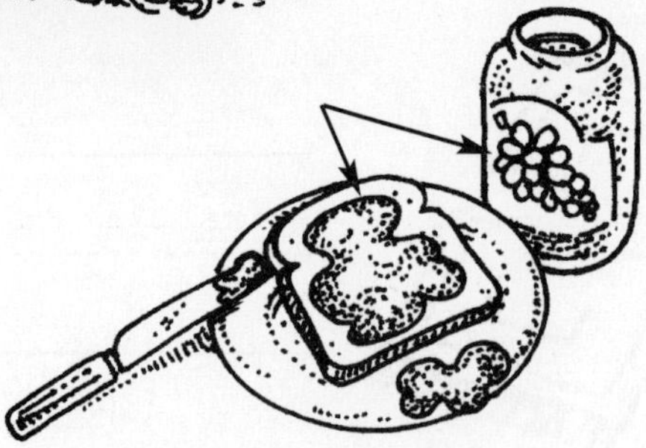

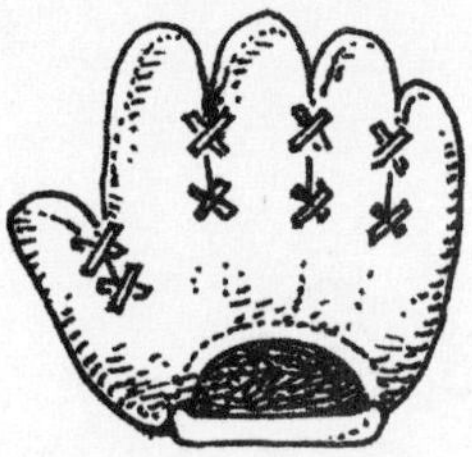

Directions: Name each picture. Color the pictures that have the short *a* sound.

Home Activity: Ask your child to name the short *a* words on this page.

Name ____________________

cat

Write.

1.  m __ n

2.  p __ g

3.  m __ t

4.  h __ t

5.  p __ d

6.  s __ n

7. 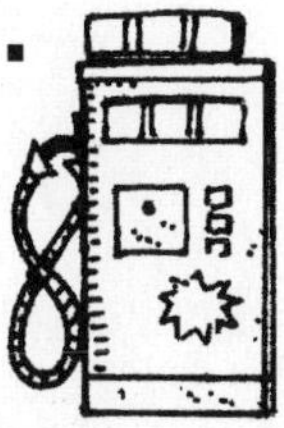 g __ s

8.  p __ n

Directions: Name each picture. Write *a* if the short *a* sound is heard.

Home Activity: Make an *a* card and have your child point to it when you say a short *a* word.

Name ______________________________

Circle.

1.  t g d

2. 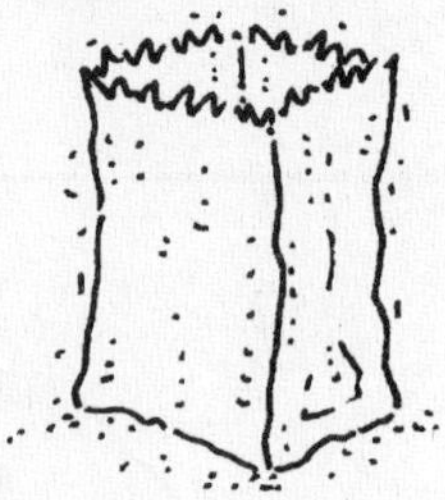 g t p

3. 

t p g

4. 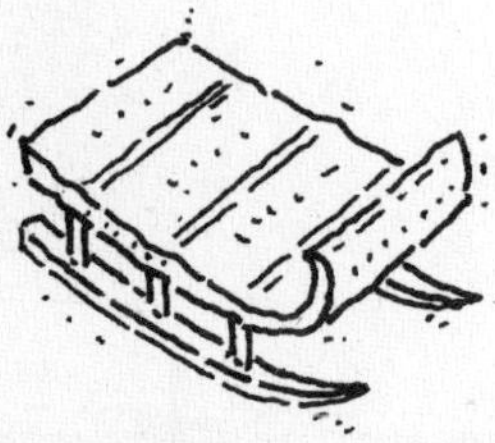 d t g

5.  p m n

6.  m n g

7. 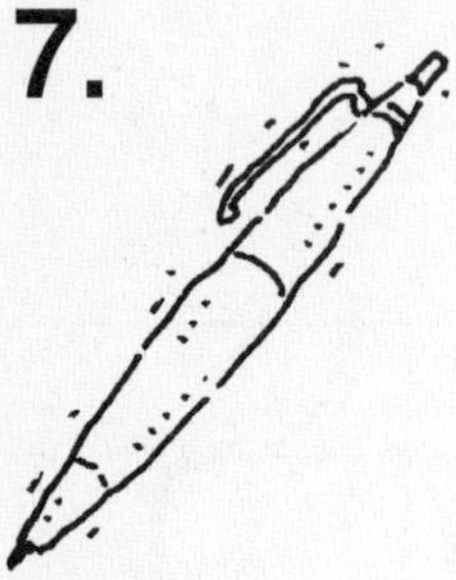 m p n

8.  p d t

9.  p g t

10.  n m t

11.  n m p

12.  m p t

Directions: Name each picture. Circle the letter that stands for the ending sound.

Home Activity: Name a letter *(n, t, d, p, g,* or *m)* and ask your child to name a word that ends with that letter.

Name ____________________

Circle.

1. r b s

2. f m r

3. r s m

4. m f r

5. m s f

6. b f r

7. b f m

8. s m r
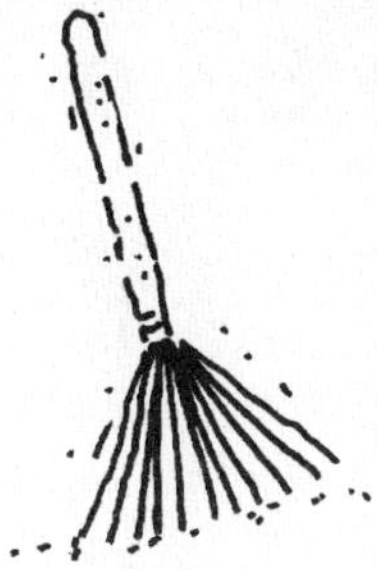

9. s b r

10. m s b
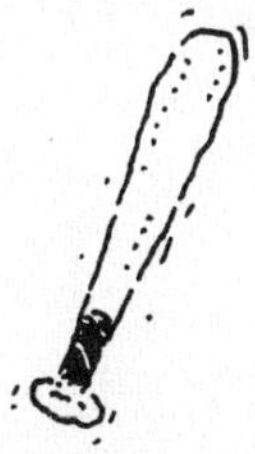

11. r s m

12. f r b

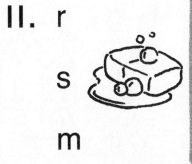

Directions: Name each picture. Circle the letter that stands for the beginning sound.

Home Activity: Point to a picture and ask your child to name another word that begins the same.

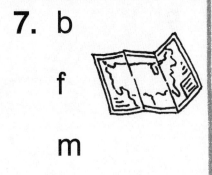

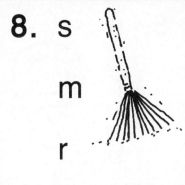

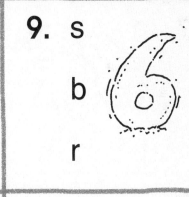

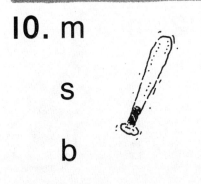

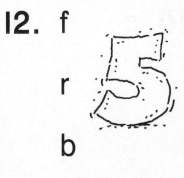

Name ______________________________

Circle.

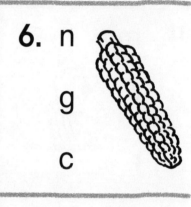

1. c t g 	**2.** t g c 	**3.** c n t 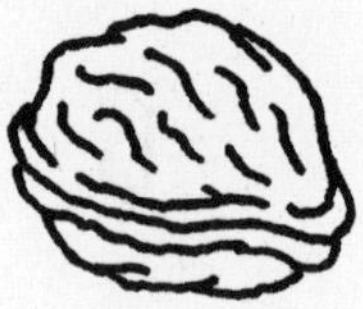
4. t g p 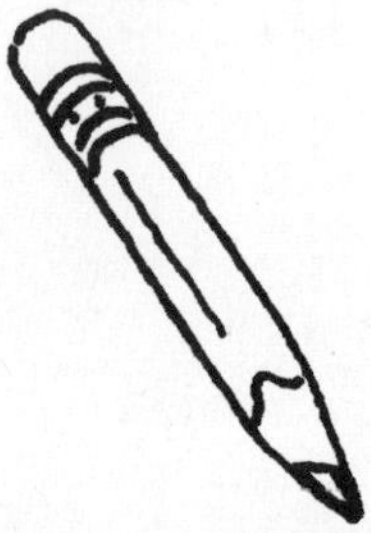	**5.** n t p 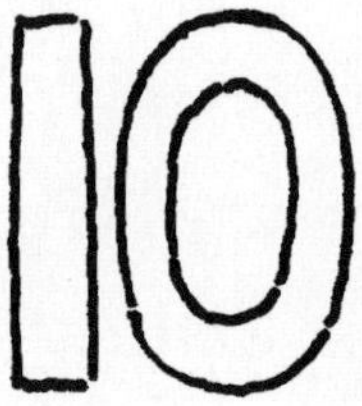	**6.** n g c 
7. g c t 	**8.** n t g 	**9.** t p n 
10. c t n 	**11.** g t c 	**12.** n g c 

Directions: Name each picture. Circle the letter that stands for the beginning sound.

Home Activity: Help your child make a picture book of things that begin with *c, g, n, p,* or *t*.

Name ______________________

Circle.

1.

hat

hit

2.

pan

pen

3.

mop

map

4.

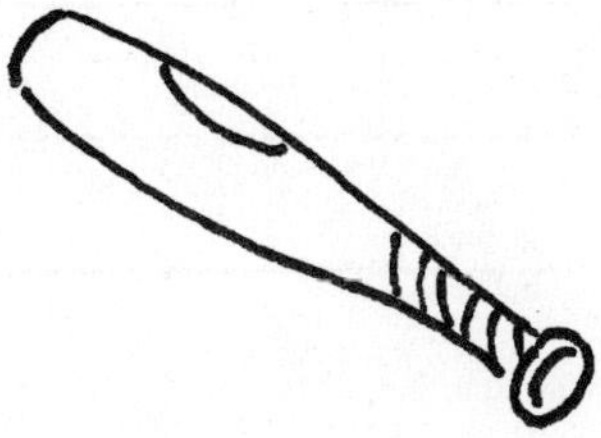

bit

bat

5.

fun

fan

6.

cab

cob

7.

cap

cup

8.

cut

cat

Directions: In each box, circle the word that names the picture.

Home Activity: Look through magazines and books for pictures of things that have the short *a* sound.

Name ______________________________

Write.

1.

2.

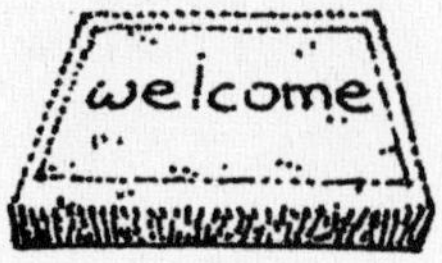

3.

4.

5.

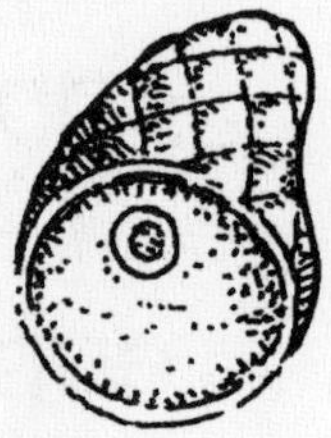

6.

7.

8.

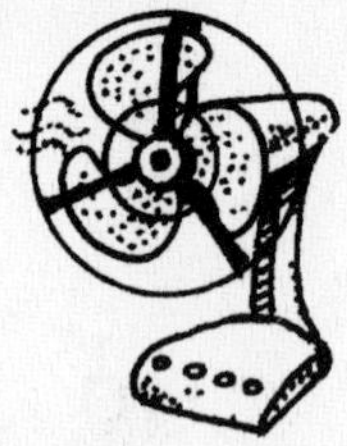

Directions: In each box, write the short *a* word for the picture name.

Home Activity: Have your child draw pictures of other short *a* words and write the word by the picture.

Name ____________________

Circle.

1.  b k s

2.  k s r

3. 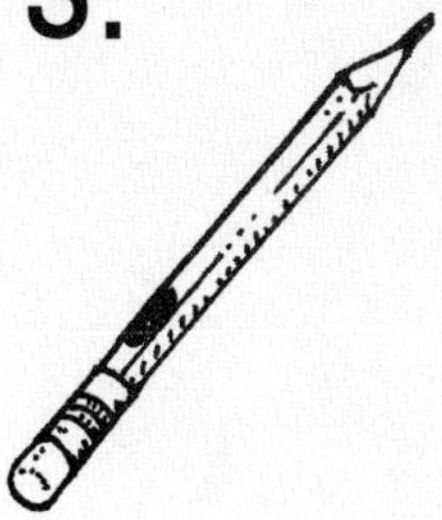 r l f

4. 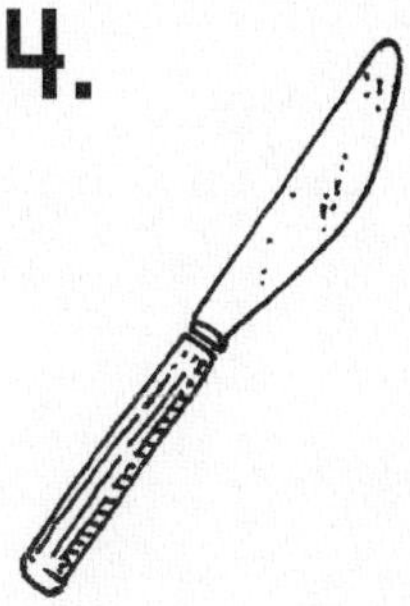 f l b

5.  l b k

6.  f b r

7. 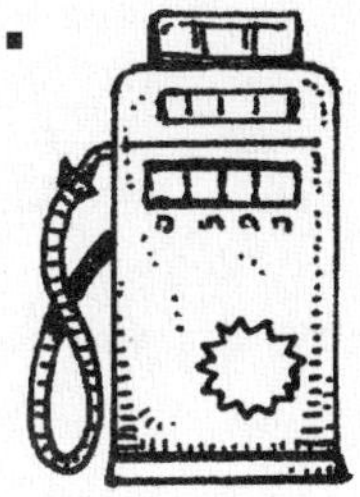 f r s

8.  r s k

9.  k b l

10. 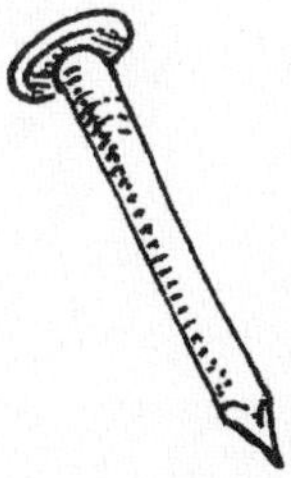 l f r

11.  s b f

12.  l r k

Directions: Name each picture. Circle the letter that stands for the ending sound.

Home Activity: Say a picture name and have your child write the letter for the ending sound.

Name ______________________

Circle.

1. d h j

2. h j k

3. k l d

4. l d h

5. k j h

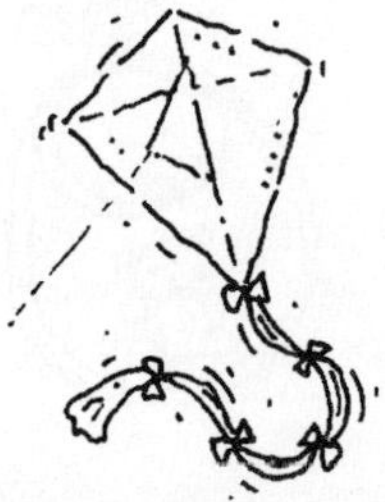

6. h d l

7. d j k

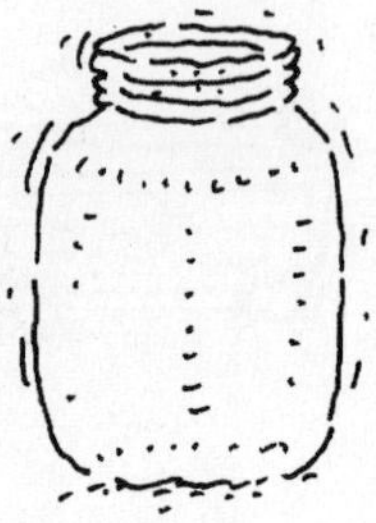

8. h j l

9. d j k

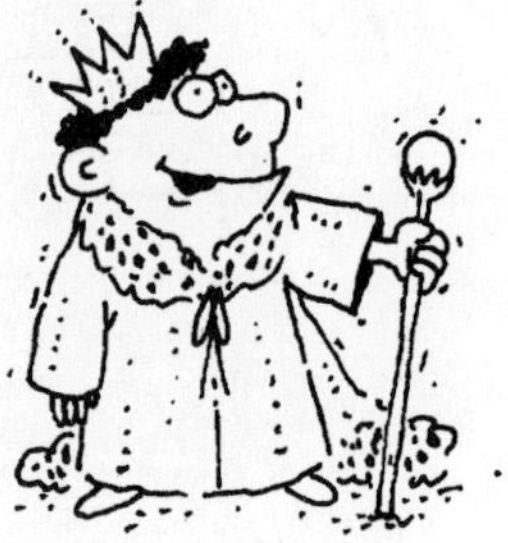

10. l j d

11. k h l

12. j d k

Directions: Name each picture. Circle the letter that stands for the beginning sound.

Home Activity: Point to a picture and ask your child to name another word that begins the same.

Name ________________________________

Circle.

1. v w y

2. w y z

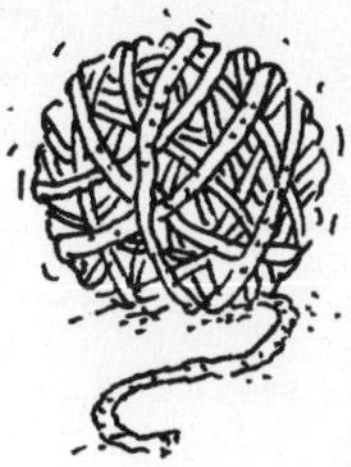

3. y z v

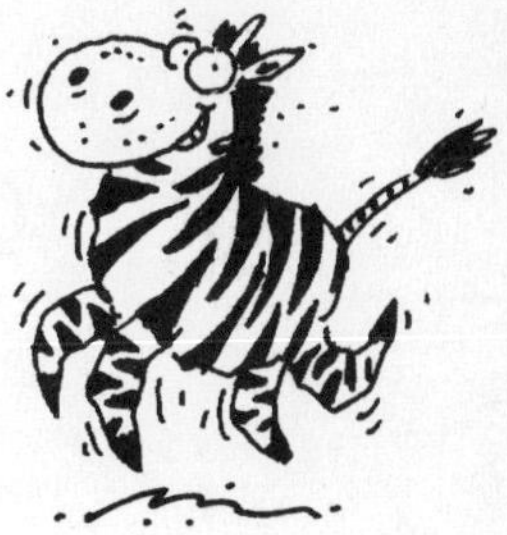

4. z v w

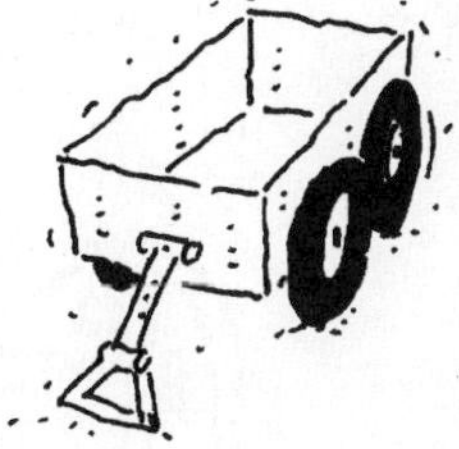

5. v z y

6. w v z

7. z y w

8. y w v

9. w v z

10. w y v

11. z v y

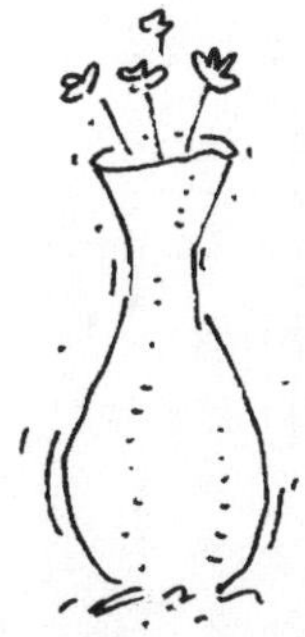

12. w v y

Directions: Name each picture. Circle the letter that stands for the beginning sound.

Home Activity: Give a clue to a picture and have your child give the word and the letter for the beginning sound.

Name ______________________________

pig

Color.

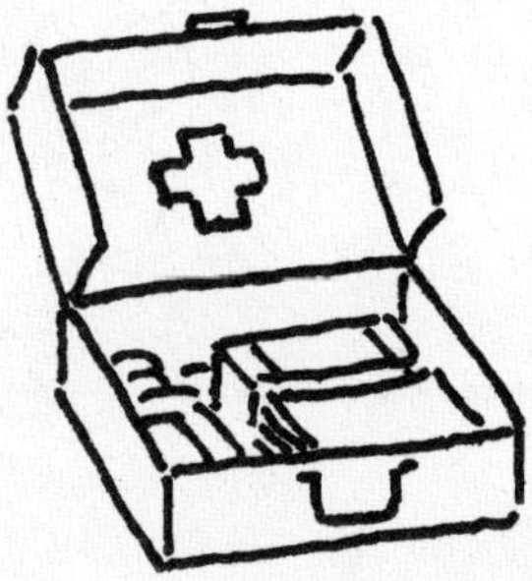

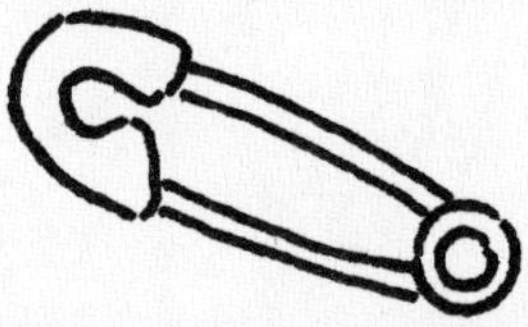

Directions: Name each picture. Color the pictures that have the short *i* sound.

Home Activity: Ask your child to name the short *i* words on this page.

Name ______________________________

pig 

Write.

1.  b b

2.  k t

3. 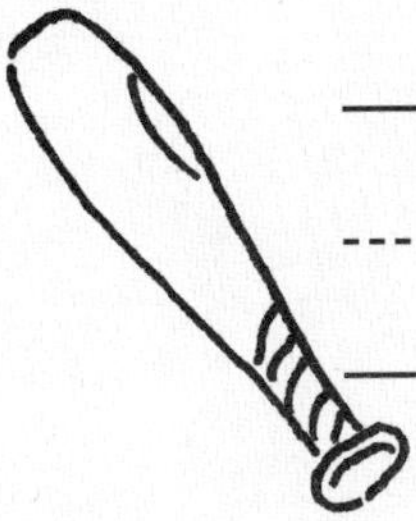 b t

4.  h t

5.  w g

6.  b g

7.  s x

8. 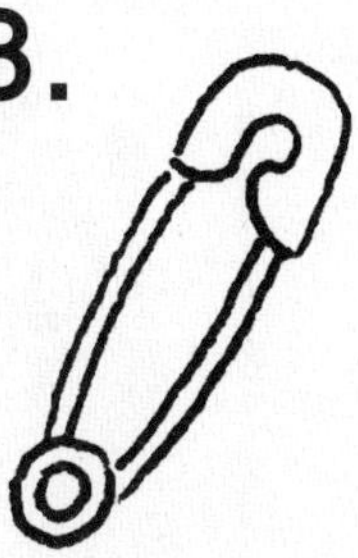 p n

Directions: Name each picture. Write *i* if the picture name has the short *i* sound.

Home Activity: Ask your child to choose a word and write a rhyming word.

Name ______________________

duck

Write.

1. 	2. 	3. 
4. 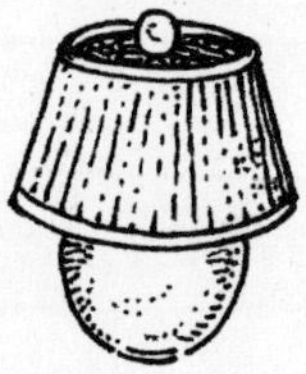	5. 	6. 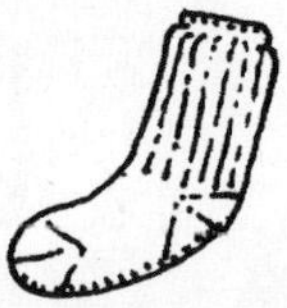
7. 	8. 	9. 
10. 	11. 	12. 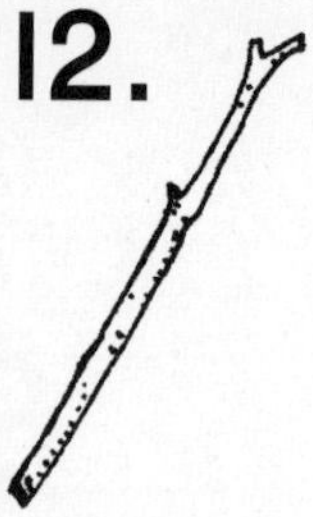

Directions: Write the letters *ck* if the picture name ends like *duck*.

Home Activity: Help your child make a list of words that end with *ck*.

Name ______________________

Circle and write.

1.

mat

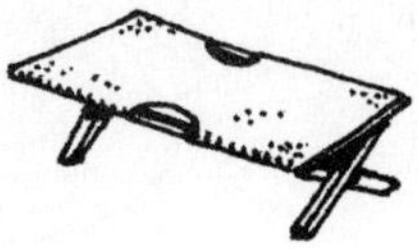

2.

can

3.

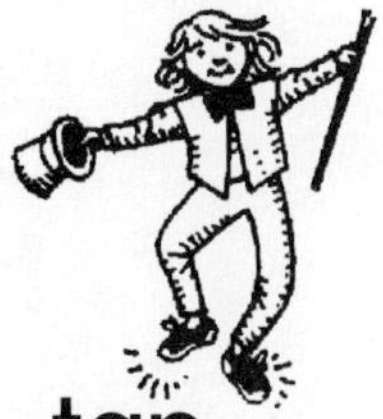

tap

4.

rag

5.

jam

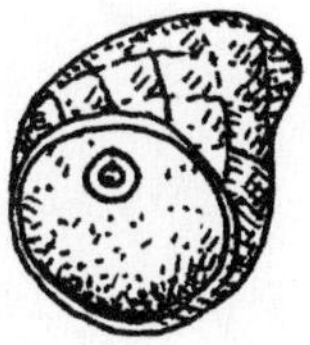

Directions: In each row, circle the picture whose name rhymes with the first word and write the word.

Home Activity: Help your child draw pictures of rhyming word pairs.

Name ______________________

Draw a line.

1.

d

2.

n

3.

t

4.

p

5.

g

6.

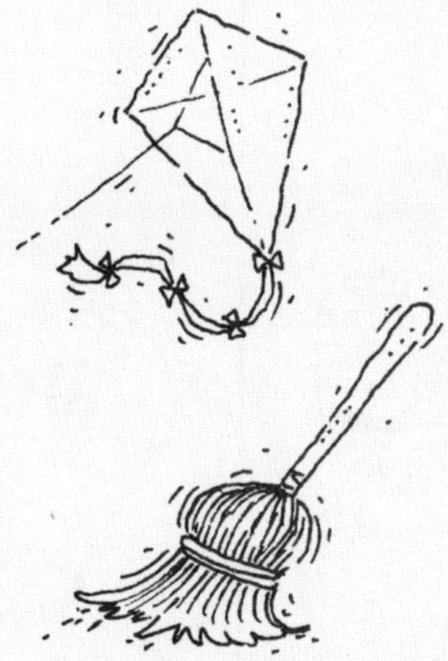

m

Directions: In each box, draw a line from the picture to the letter for the ending sound.

Home Activity: Say a word and ask your child to name the letter for the ending sound.

Name ______________________________

Circle.

1.

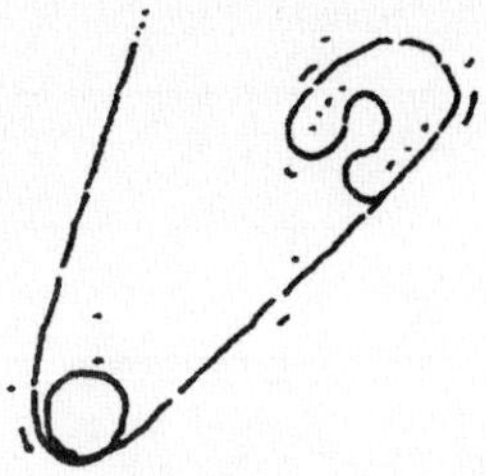

pin

pan

2.

fan

fin

3.

hot

hit

4.

dig

dog

5.

peg

pig

6.

had

hid

7.

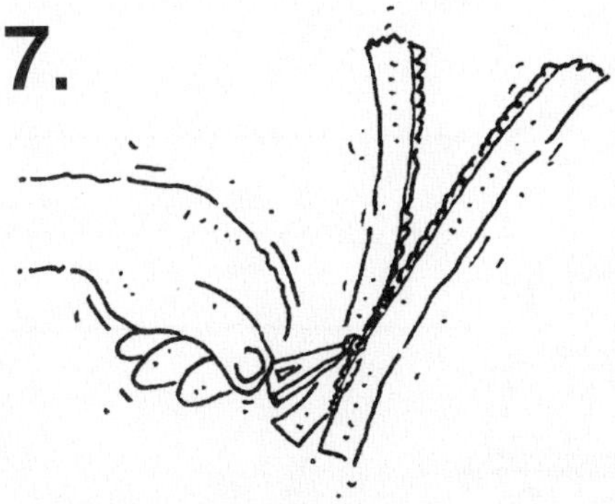

zip

zap

8.

bug

big

Directions: In each box, circle the word that names the picture.

Home Activity: Say a short *i* word and have your child write the word.

Name ______________________

Write.

1.

2.

3.

4.

5.

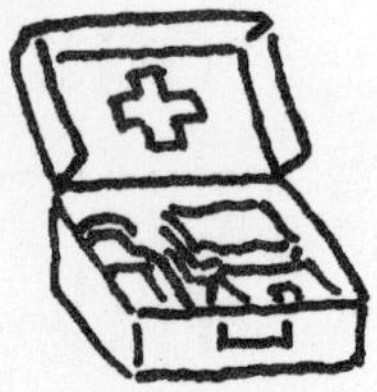

6.

7.

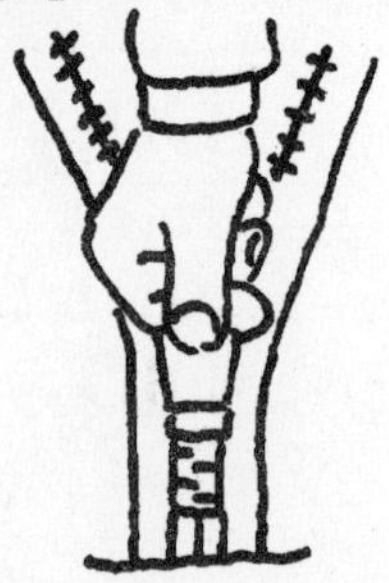

8.

Directions: In each box, write the short *i* word that names the picture.

Home Activity: Point to a word and ask your child to name a rhyming word.

Name ______________________________

x

Write.

1.

2.

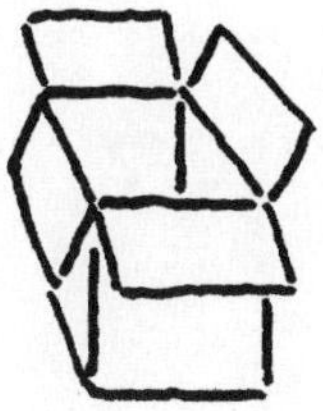

3.

4.

5.

6.

7.

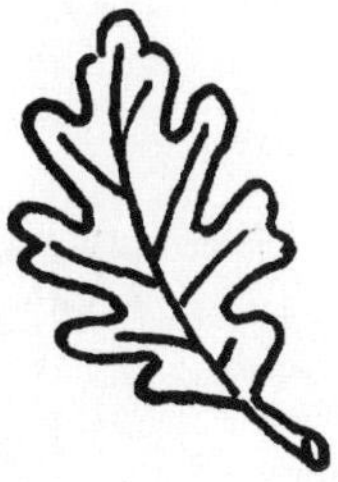

8.

9.

Directions: Write the letter *x* if the picture name ends like *fox*.

Home Activity: Help your child make a list of words that end with *x*.

Name ______________________________

Draw lines.

1.  pan

2. 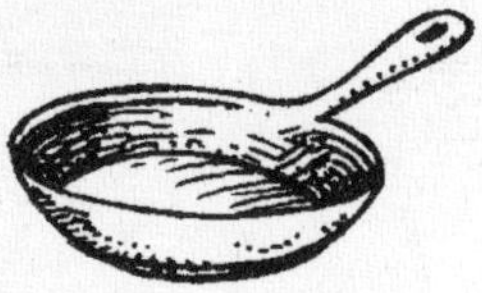 map

3.  cat

4.  man

5.  bat

6. 

mat

7.  gas

8.  bag

9.  cab

10.  rag

Directions: Draw a line from the picture to the word that tells about the picture.

Home Activity: Say a picture name and have your child spell the word.

Name ______________________________

Draw a line.

1.

b

2.

r

3.

k

4.

f

5.

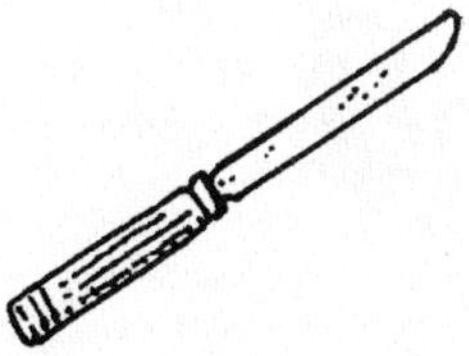

s

6.

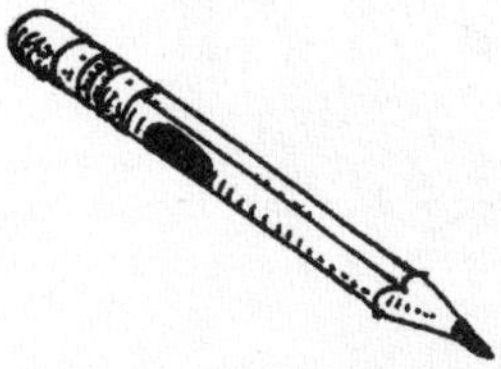

l

Directions: In each box, draw a line from the picture to the letter for the ending sound.

Home Activity: Help your child make a page showing pictures and the letter for the ending sound.

Name ______________________________

fox

Color.

Directions: Name each picture. Color the pictures that have the short *o* sound.

Home Activity: Ask your child to name the short *o* words on this page.

Name ______________________________

fox

Write.

1.
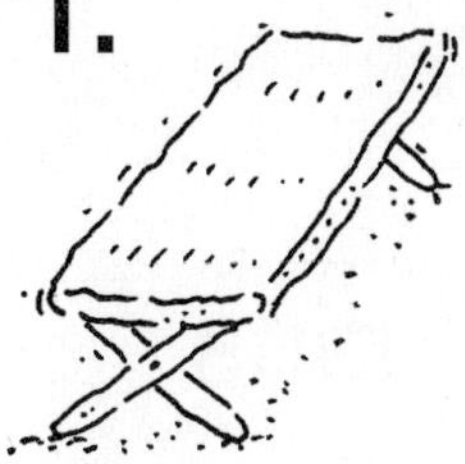

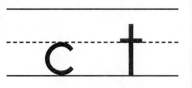

c t

2.
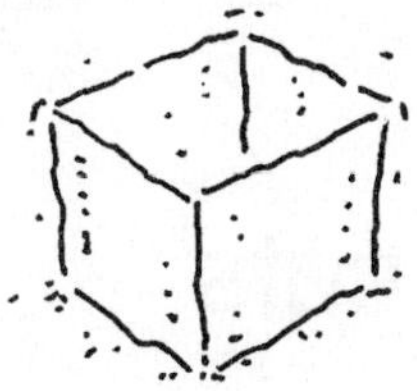

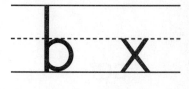

b x

3.
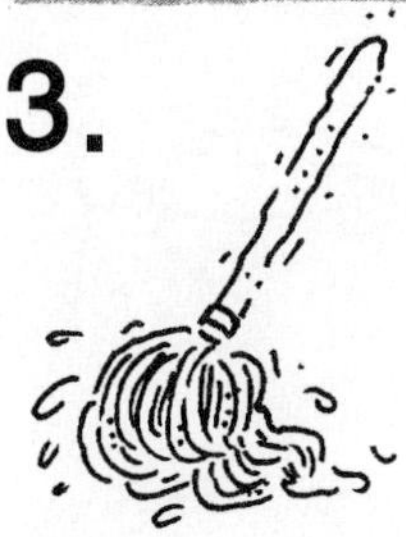

m p

4.

h t

5.

c p

6.

t p

7.

c b

8.
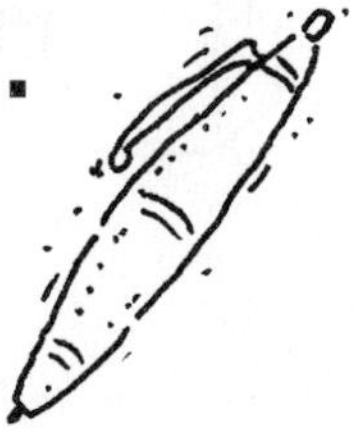

p n

Directions: Name each picture. Write *o* if the short *o* sound is heard.

Home Activity: Help your child look in magazines or newspapers to find short *o* words.

Name ______________________________

Draw lines.

1.

cat cats

2.

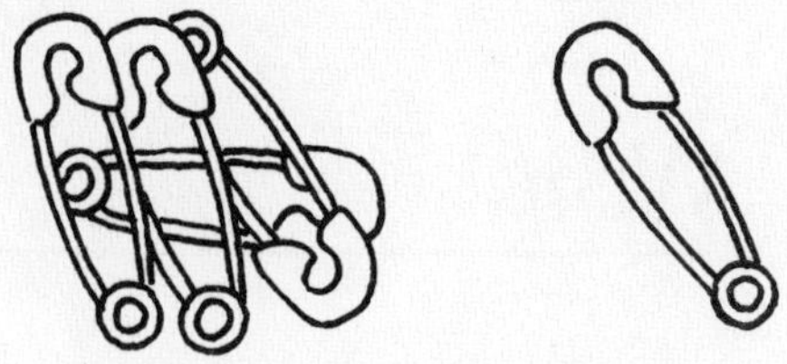

pin pins

3.

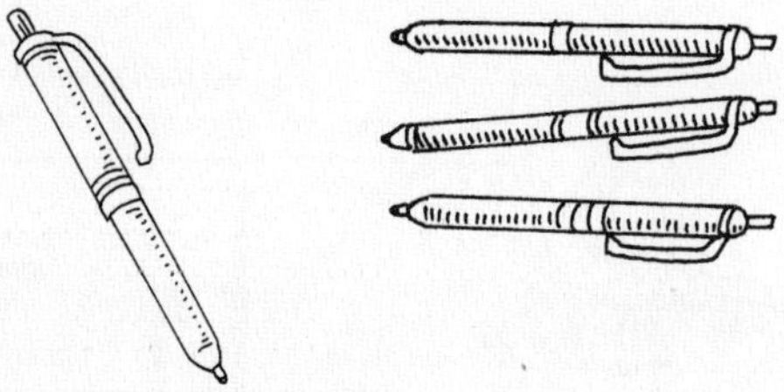

pen pens

4.

car cars

5.

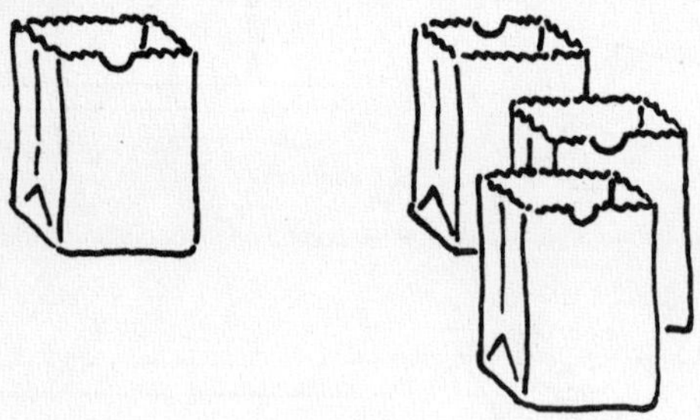

bag bags

6.

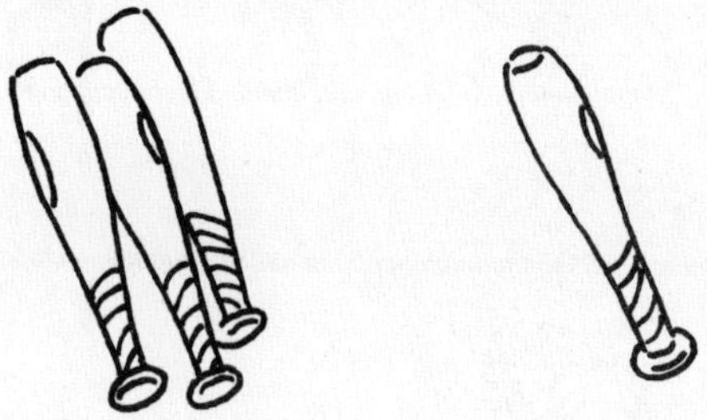

bat bats

Directions: In each box, draw a line from the picture to the word that tells how many.

Home Activity: Have your child name things in your home giving the singular and the plural forms of the word.

Name ____________________

Circle and write.

1. 
dig

2. 
fin
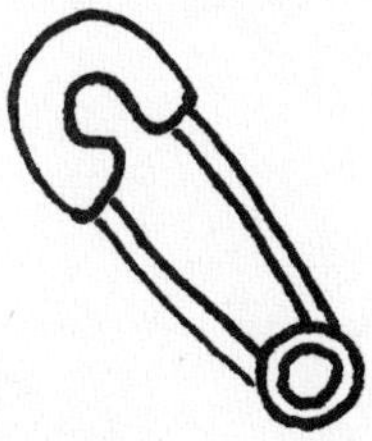

3. 
kit

4. 
big

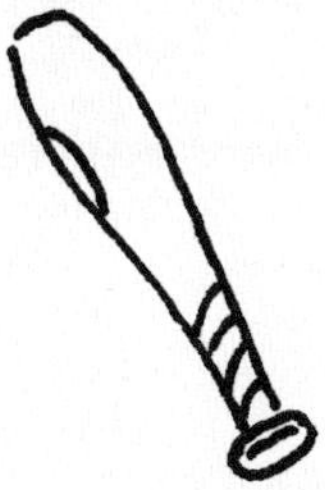

5. 
mix

Directions: In each row, circle the picture whose name rhymes with the word and write the picture name.

Home Activity: Work with your child to make a list of rhyming short *i* words.

Name ______________________________

Draw a line.

1.

X

2.

X

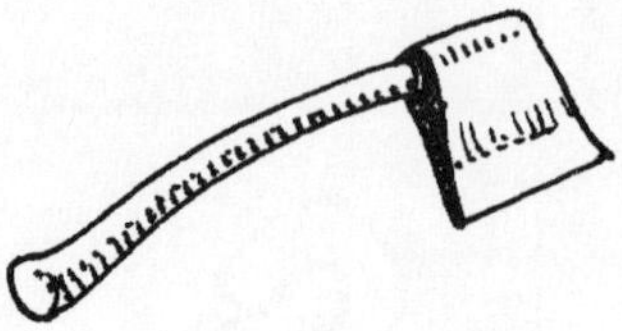

3.

X

4.

X

5.

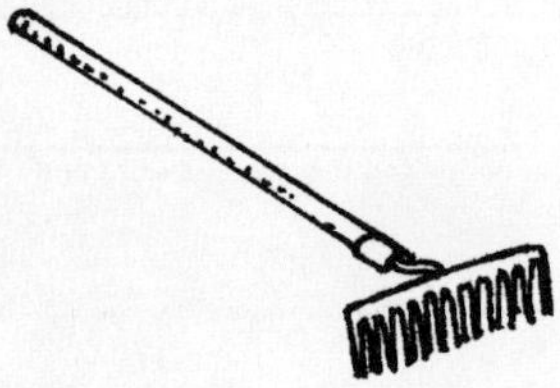

X

6.

X

Directions: In each box, draw a line from the picture to the letter for the ending sound.

Home Activity: Help your child use each *x* word in a sentence.

Name ______________________

Circle.

1.

tap

top

2.

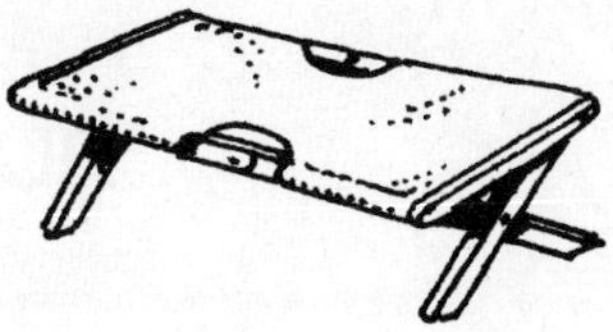

cot

cat

3.

lock

lick

4.

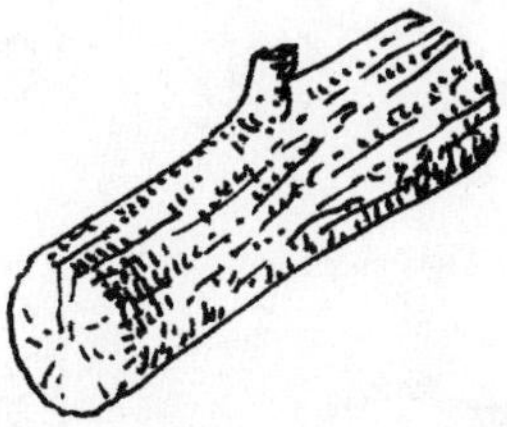

leg

log

5.

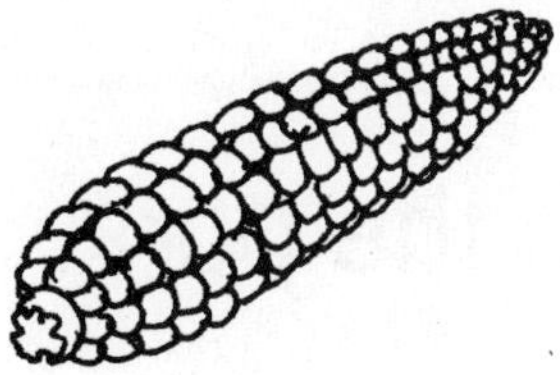

cob

cab

6.

map

mop

7.

pop

pep

8.

fix

fox

Directions: In each box, circle the word that names the picture.

Home Activity: Read a story and ask your child to listen for short *o* words.

Name ______________________________

Circle.

1. 

Tara _____ very fast.

hop hops

2. 

Jill can _____ Jan.

tag tags

3. 

Sara _____ the ball and runs.

hit hits

4. 

Tim can _____ in the park.

jog jogs

5. 

Rob _____ out a leaf for us.

cut cuts

Directions: In each row, circle the word that completes the sentence.

Home Activity: Read sentences from a story and have your child name the action word in each sentence.

Name ____________________

Write.

1.  call + ing = ____________________

2.  play + ing = ____________________

3.  look + ing = ____________________

4.  help + ing = ____________________

5.  walk + ing = ____________________

Directions: Add the ending and write the new word.

Home Activity: Help your child look for words with *-ing*.

Name ______________________________

Draw lines.

1. 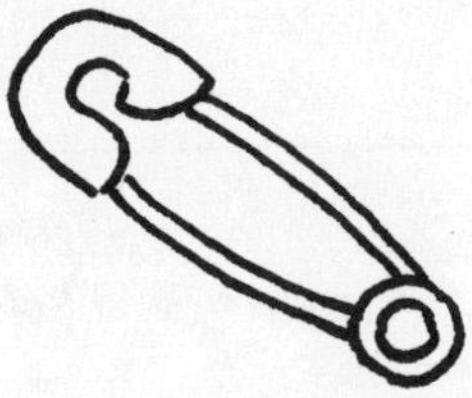 pig

2.  pin

3. 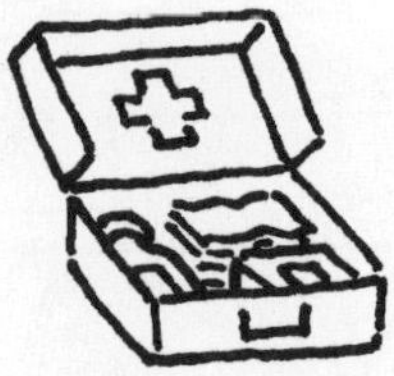 kit

4.  lid

5.  six

6.  hit

7.  zip

8. 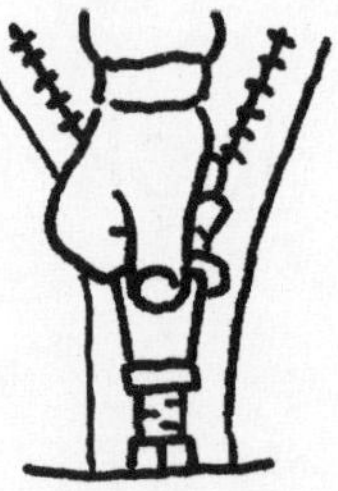 bib

9.  big

10.  wig

Directions: Draw a line from the picture to the word that tells about the picture.

Home Activity: Help your child make a list of other short *i* words.

Name ______________________________

Draw a line.

1.

ck

2.

ck

3.

ck

4.

ck

5.

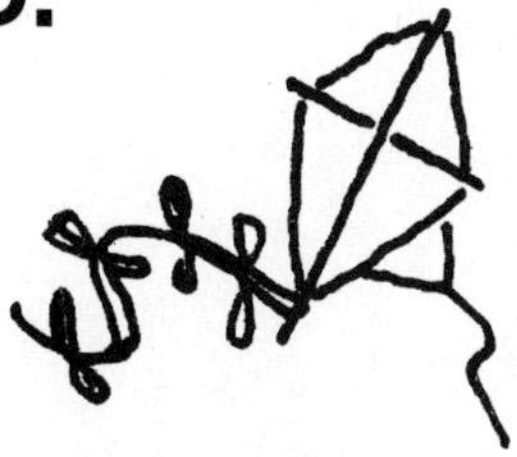

ck

6.

ck

Directions: In each box, draw a line from the picture to the letters for the ending sound.

Home Activity: Help your child write the *ck* words for the pictures on the page.

Name ______________________________

bell

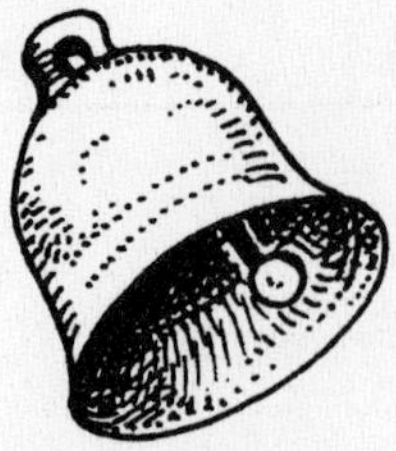

Color.

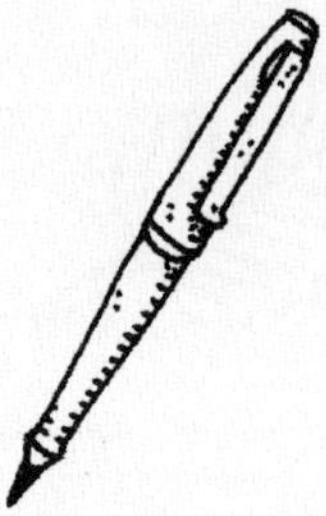

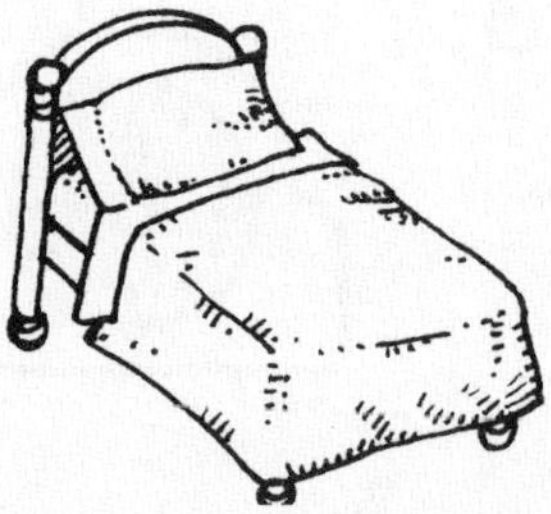

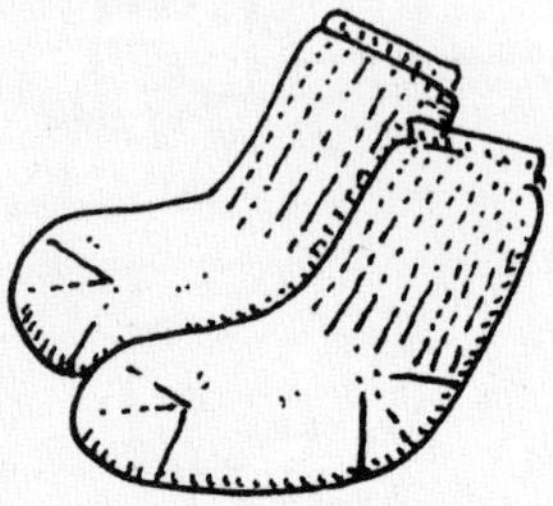

Directions: Name each picture. Color the pictures that have the short *e* sound.

Home Activity: Help your child make a short *e* picture collection by looking for short *e* pictures in magazines.

Name ____________________

bell

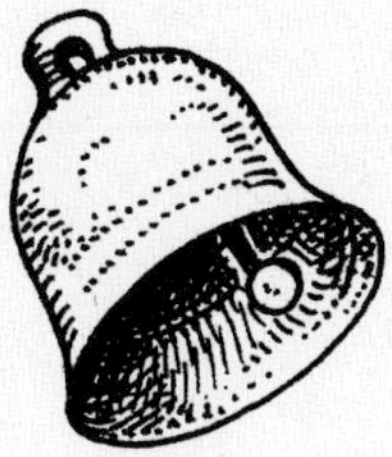

Write.

1.

h n

2.

j t

3.

b d

4.
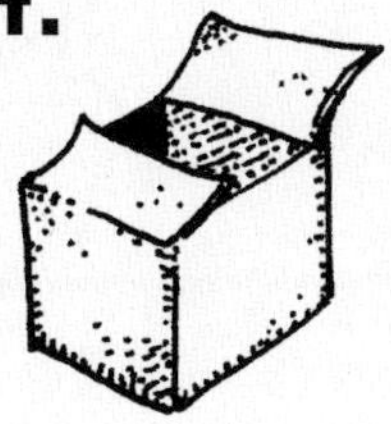
b x

5.
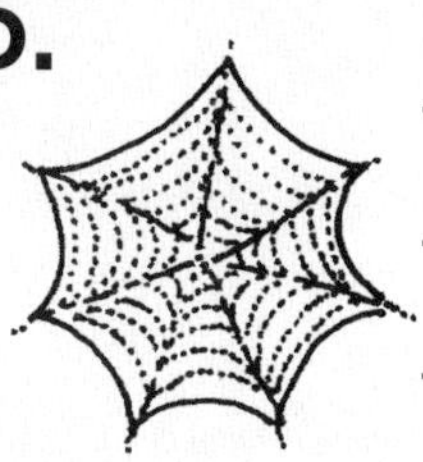
w b

6.

t n

7.

b s

8.
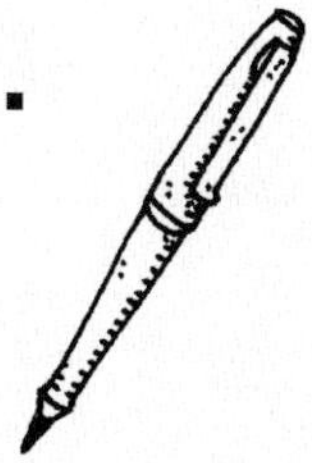
p n

Directions: Name each picture. Write *e* if the short *e* sound is heard.

Home Activity: Make a set of word cards with short *e* words. Help your child read the words.

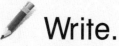

Name ______________________________

Circle.

1. 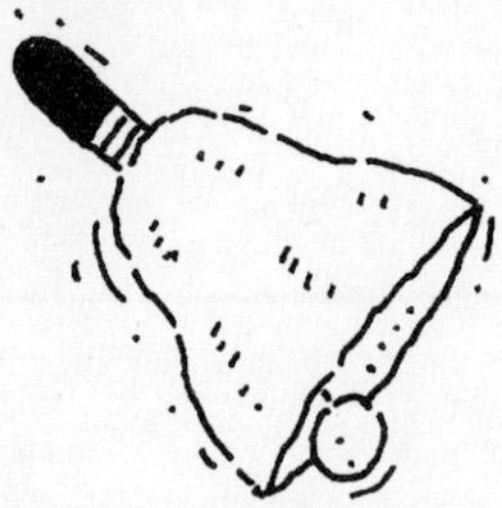

ll

ss

2. 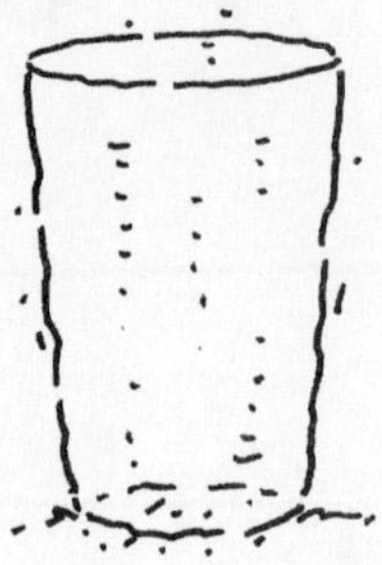

ff

ss

3. 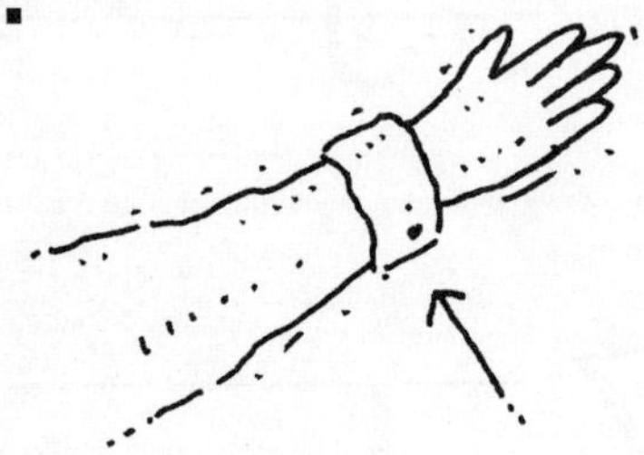

ff

ll

4. 

ll

ss

5. 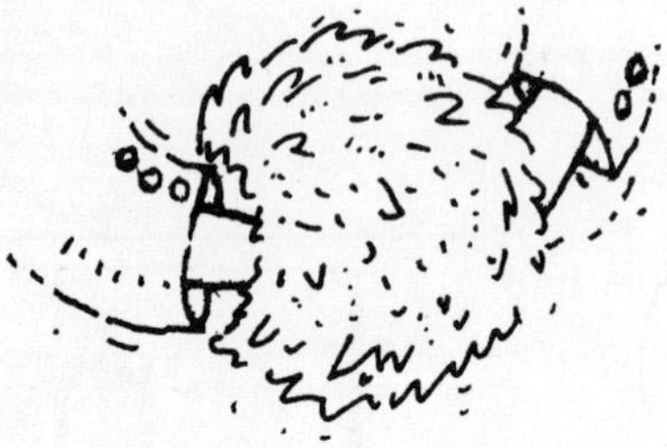

ss

ff

6. 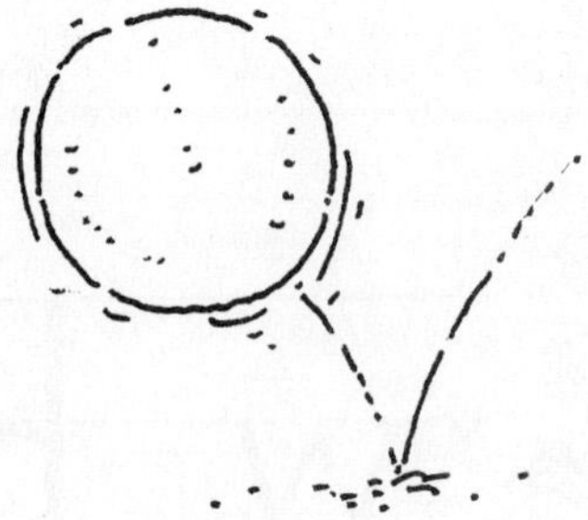

ff

ll

7. 

ll

ss

8. 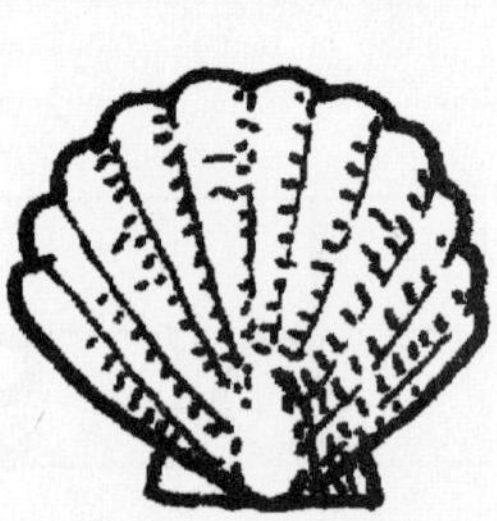

ff

ll

Directions: Name each picture. Circle the letters that stand for the ending sound.

Home Activity: Help your child make a list of words that end with *ll*, *ss*, and *ff*.

Name ______________________

Circle and write.

1. 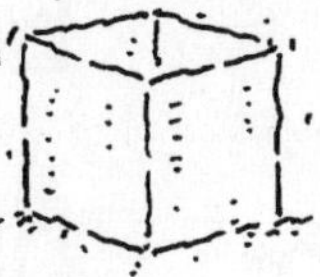
box

2. 
mop

3. 
dot

4. 
clock

5. 
hot

Directions: In each row, circle the picture whose name rhymes with the word and write the picture name.

Home Activity: Help your child make a list of rhyming words for *mop* and *cot*.

Name ______________________

Circle and write.

1. 

cat

cats

2. 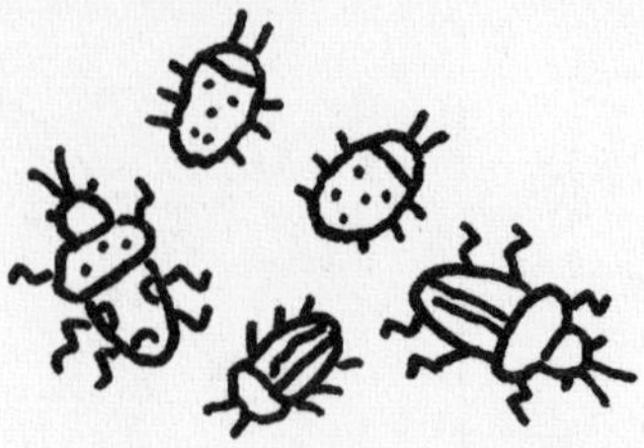

bug

bugs

3. 

duck

ducks

4. 

dog

dogs

5. 

pig

pigs

6. 

hen

hens

Directions: Circle the word that names the picture. Write the word.

Home Activity: Name an object and have your child tell the word that means more than one.

Name ______________________________

Circle.

1.
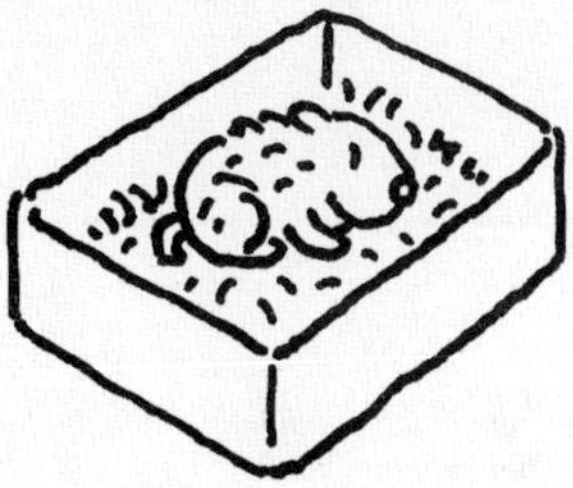
pet
pot

2.
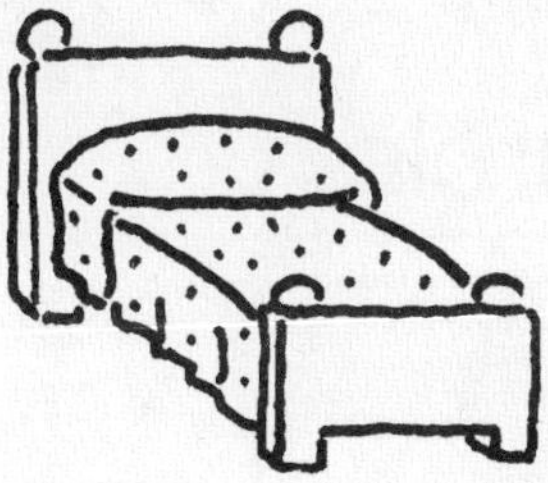
bad
bed

3.
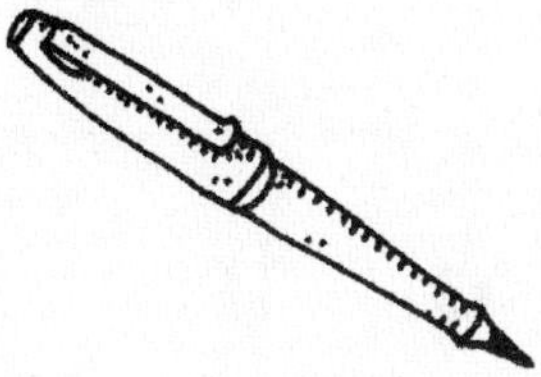
pan
pen

4.
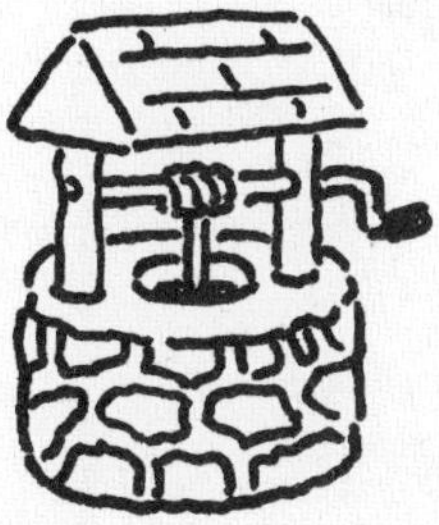
well
wall

5.
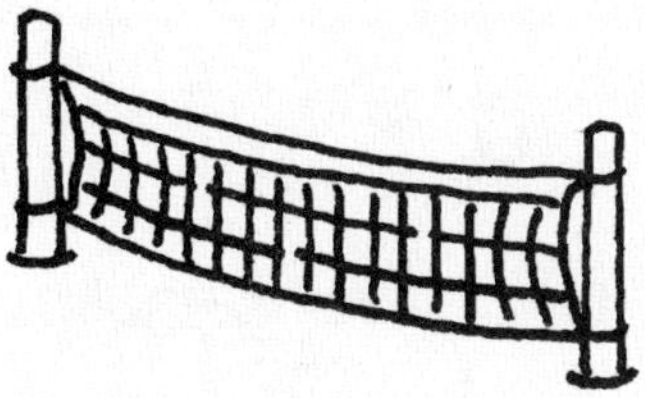
not
net

6.
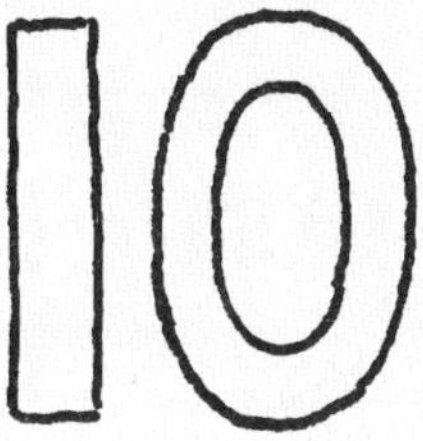
ten
tan

7.
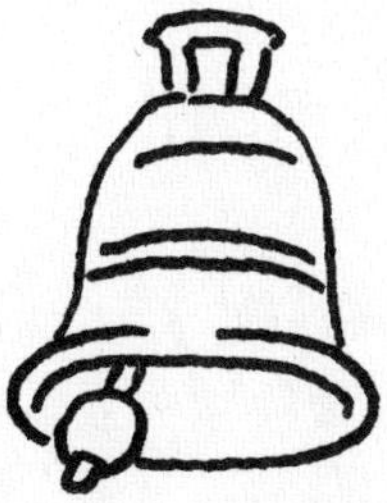
ball
bell

8.
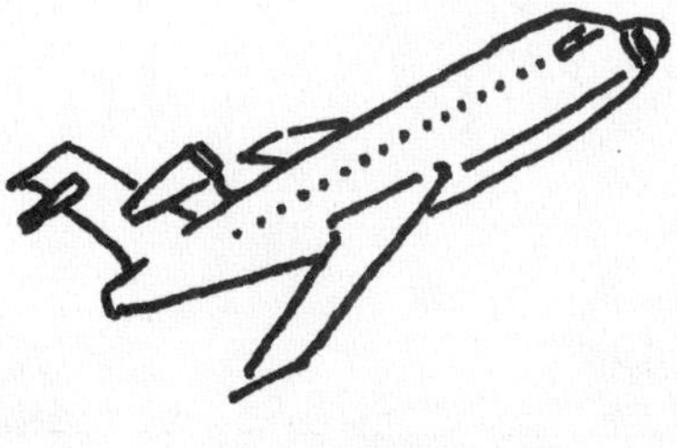
jot
jet

Directions: In each box, circle the word that names the picture.

Home Activity: Say a word from the page and have your child point to the word.

Name ______________________________

br  tr 

Circle.

1. br tr 	**2.** dr tr 	**3.** dr gr 
4. gr fr 	**5.** fr br 	**6.** tr br 
7. tr dr 	**8.** gr dr 	**9.** tr fr 
10. fr br 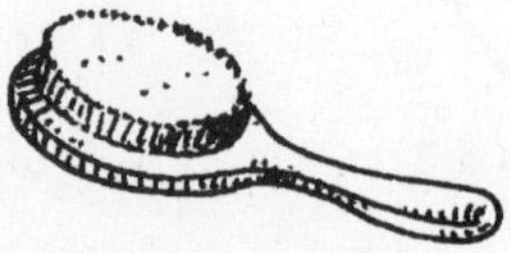	**11.** br tr 	**12.** tr dr 

Directions: Name each picture. Circle the letters that stand for the beginning sound.

Home Activity: Point to a picture and ask your child to name another word that begins the same.

Name ______________________________

fl  gl 

 Circle.

1. sl bl 	2. gl bl 	3. fl gl 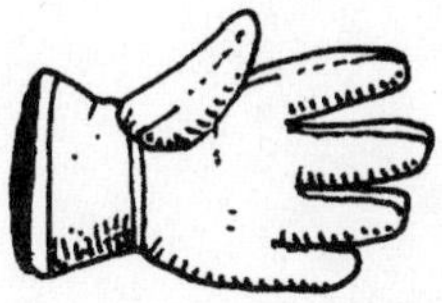
4. fl cl 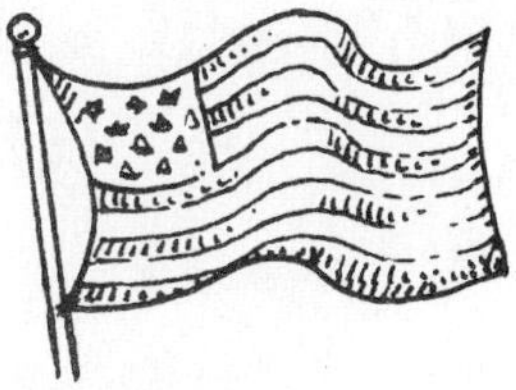	5. pl cl 	6. pl sl 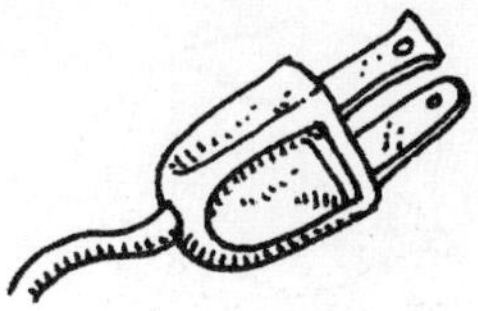
7. bl sl 	8. fl gl 	9. gl fl 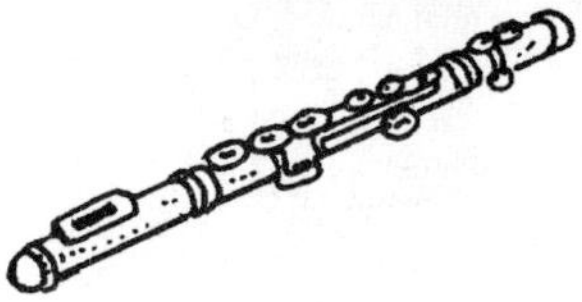
10. fl cl 	11. pl cl 	12. gl sl 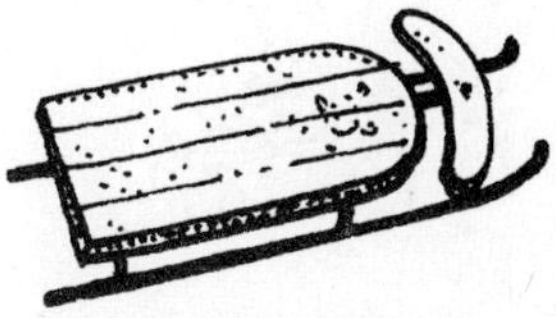

 **Directions:** Name each picture. Circle the letters that stand for the beginning sound.

 **Home Activity:** Say a word from the page and ask your child to write the letters for the beginning sound.

Name ______________________________

Draw lines.

1.  box

2.  hop

3. 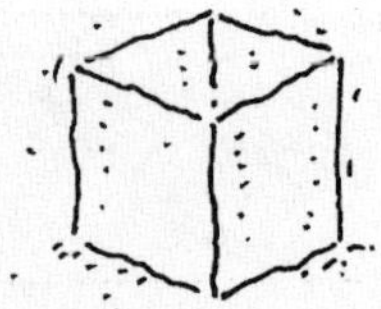 dot

4.  mop

5.  pot

6.  top

7.  cot

8.  fox

9.  lock

10.  pop

Directions: Draw a line from the picture to the word that tells about the picture.

Home Activity: Have your child name pairs of rhyming words from the pictures on the page.

Name ______________________

Circle.

1. 

I ____.

win wins

2. 

I can ____.

run runs

3. 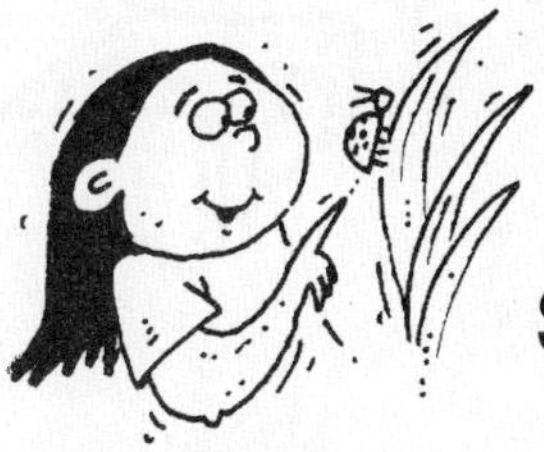

Teri ____ the bug.

see sees

4. 

Will José ____ it?

hit hits

5. 

I will ____ that pet.

get gets

Directions: In each row, circle the word that completes the sentence. Write the word.

Home Activity: Have your child use each answer word in a sentence.

Name ______________________________

duck

Color.

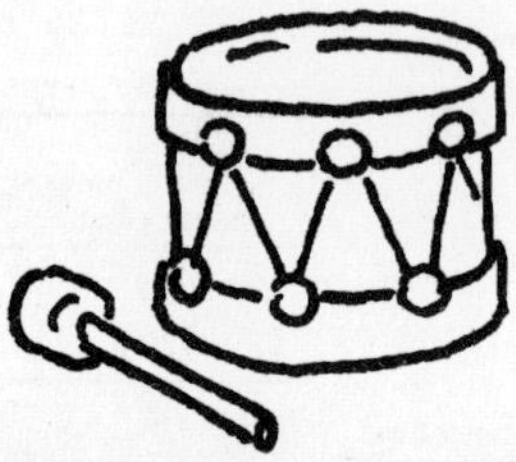

Directions: Name each picture. Color the pictures that have the short *u* sound.

Home Activity: Have your child write these short *u* words: *run, cut, fun*.

Name ______________________________

duck 

Write.

1.  c p

2.  b s

3. 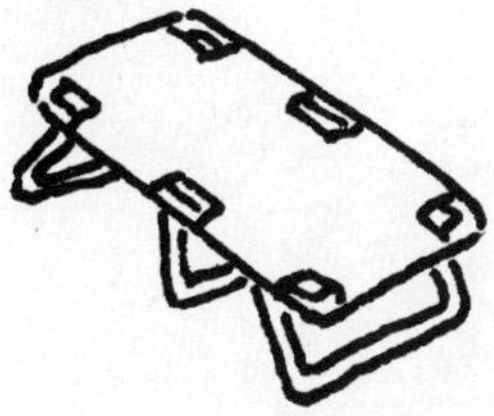 c t

4.  b g

5. 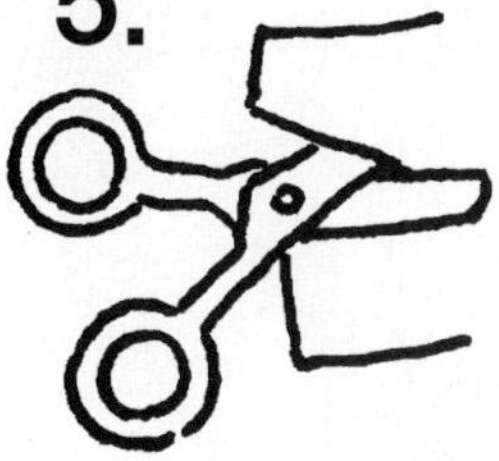 c t

6.  b d

7.  s n

8.  t b

Directions: Name each picture. Write *u* if the short *u* sound is heard.

Home Activity: Point to a word and have your child change the vowel to make a new word—*cup, cap.*

Name ______________________

st 

sk 

Circle.

1. st sp

2. sn sp

3. sk sn
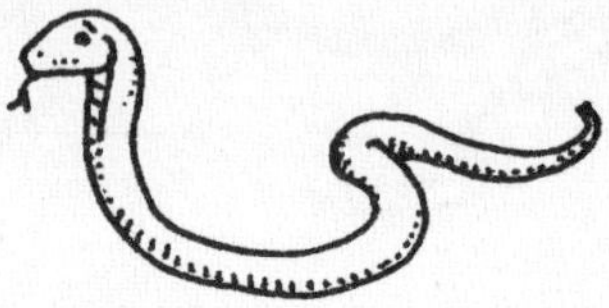

4. sk sw
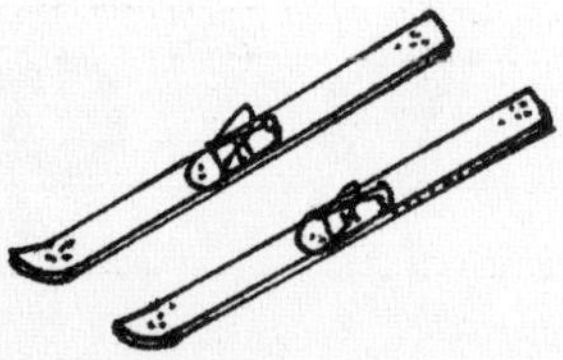

5. st sw

6. st sp

7. sp sn
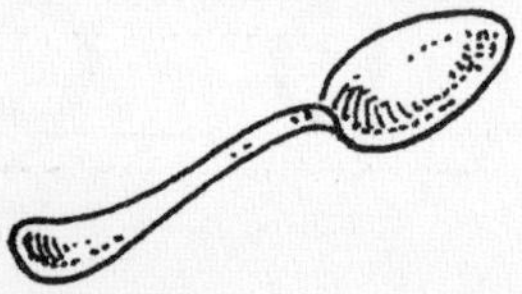

8. sn sk

9. sw sk

10. sw st

11. st sp

12. sp sn
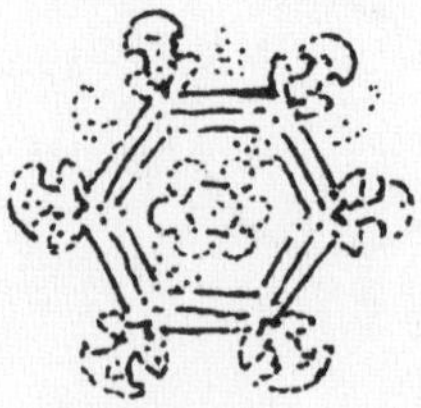

Directions: Name each picture. Circle the letters that stand for the beginning sound.

Home Activity: Write *st, sp, sn, sk,* and *sw* on paper. Help your child draw pictures of words that begin with each blend.

Name ______________________________

Circle and write.

1\. 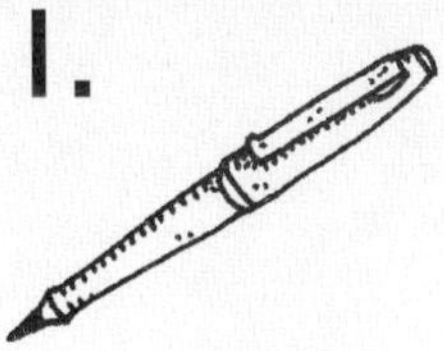
pen

2\. 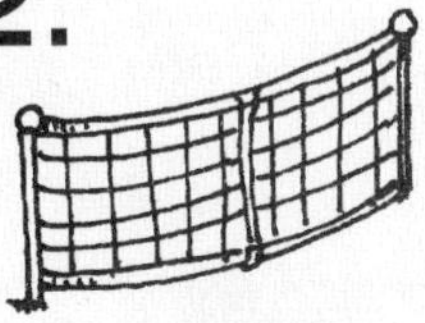
net

3\. 
bell

4\. 
pet

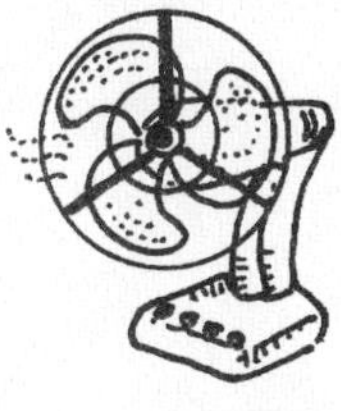 

5\. 
fed

Directions: In each row, circle the picture whose name rhymes with the word and write the picture name.

Home Activity: Write these words and ask your child to change them to short *e* words: *log (leg), man (men), got (get), sat (set).*

Name ______________________________

Draw a line.

1.

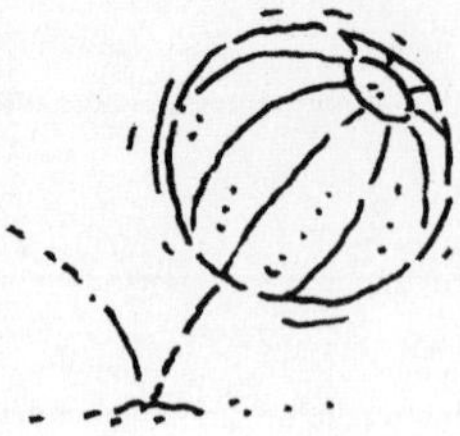

ll

2.

ss

3.

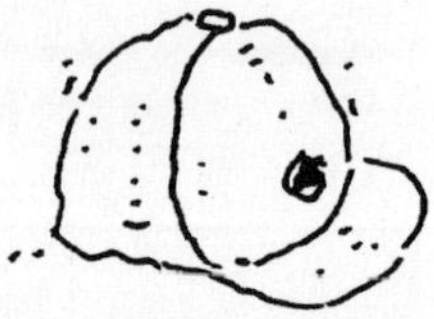

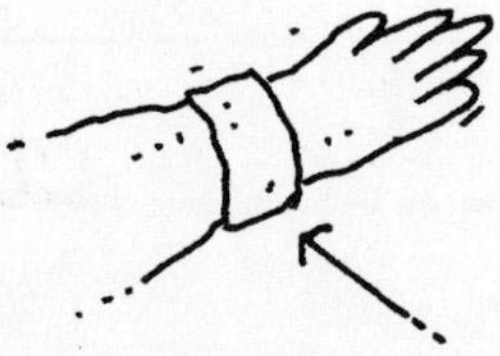

ff

4.

ll

5.

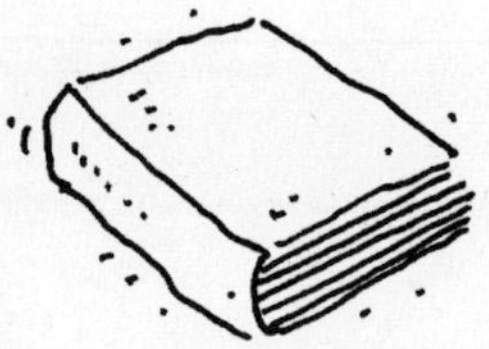

ss

6.

ff

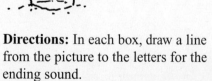

Directions: In each box, draw a line from the picture to the letters for the ending sound.

Home Activity: Say the *ll, ss, ff* words and ask your child which double consonant is at the end of each word.

Name ______________________________

Circle.

1.

cap

cup

2.

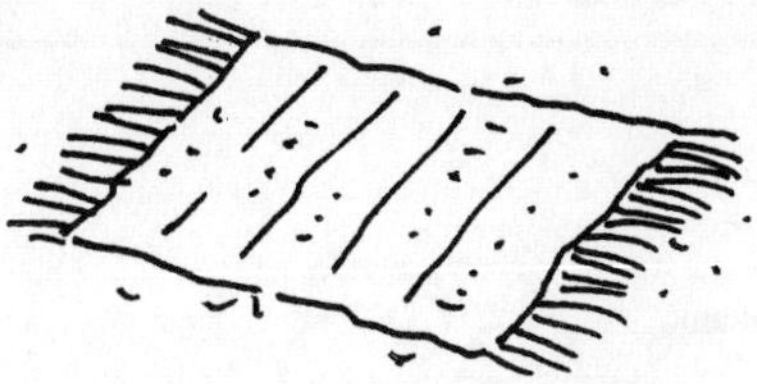

rug

rig

3.

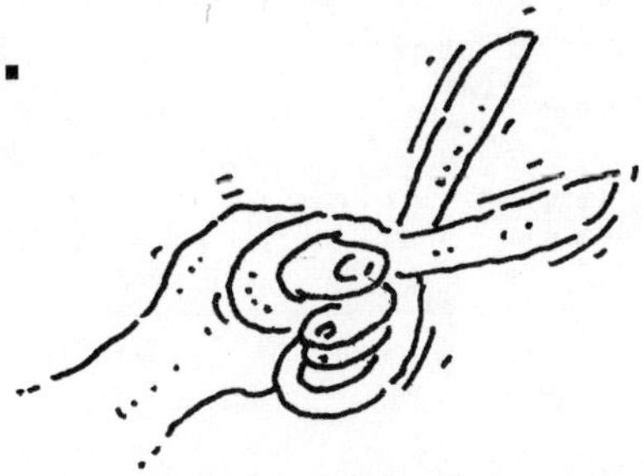

cat

cut

4.

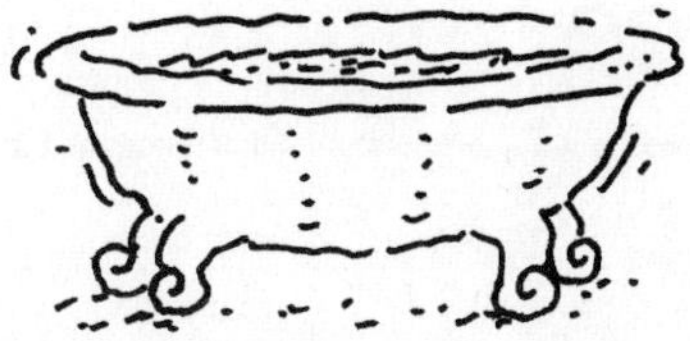

tab

tub

5.

bug

big

6.

cob

cub

7.

pep

pup

8.

not

nut

Directions: In each box, circle the word that names the picture.

Home Activity: Say a picture name and ask your child to write the word.

Name ______________________________

city c = /s/ cat c = /k/

Circle.

1\.

k

s

mice

2\.

k

s

cube

3\.

k

s

pencil

4\.

k

s

cent

5\.

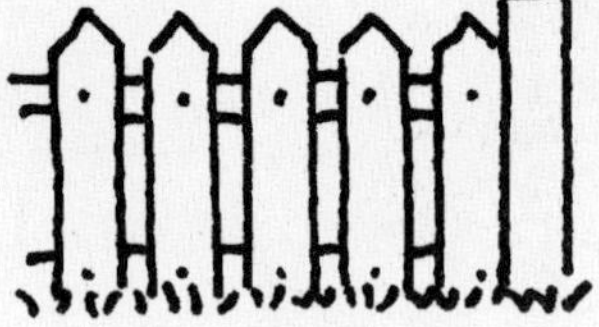

k

s

fence

6\.

k

s

music

Directions: Circle the letter that tells what sound *c* stands for in the picture name.

Home Activity: Help your child make a list of words in which *c* stands for the *s* sound.

Name ______________________________

giant g = /j/ goat g = /g/

Circle.

1.

g

j

cage

2.

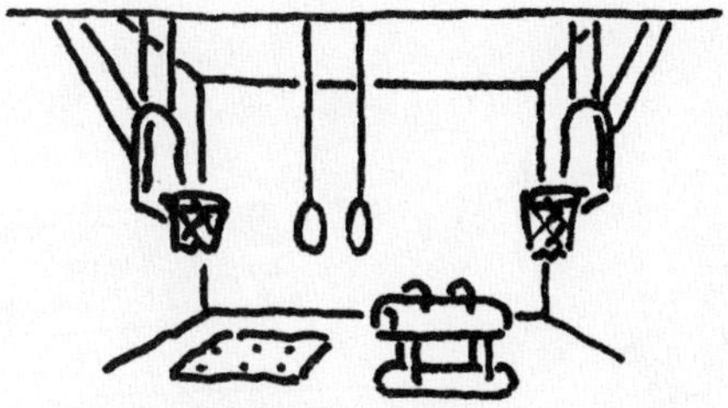

g

j

gym

3.

g

j

giraffe

4.

g

j

gate

5.

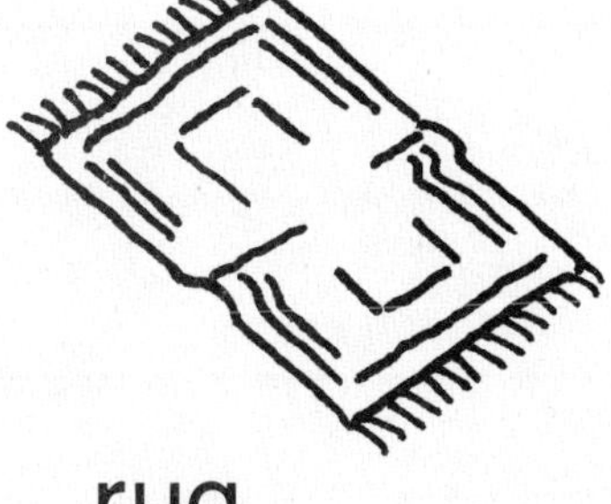

g

j

rug

6.

g

j

gem

Directions: Circle the letter that tells what sound *g* stands for in the picture name.

Home Activity: Read *g* words from the dictionary. Ask your child to identify words in which *g* stands for /j/.

Name ________________________

bag  2 bags 

Write.

1. rug 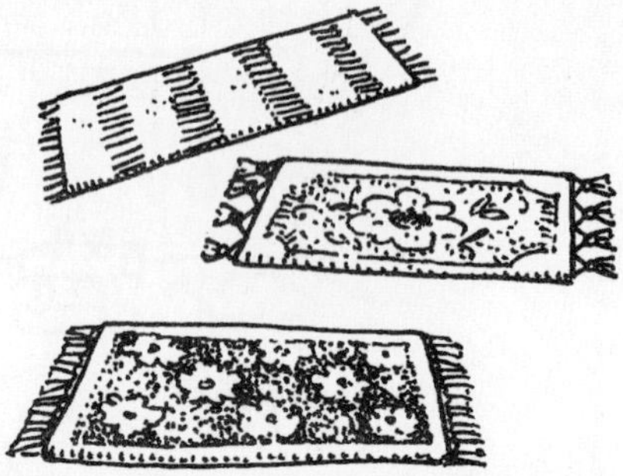

2. pen 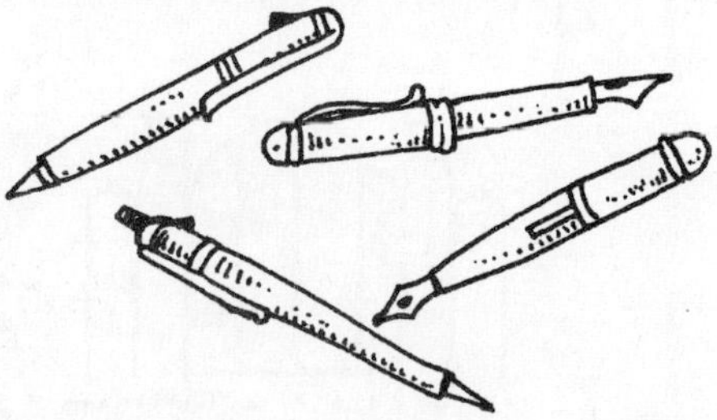

3. pan 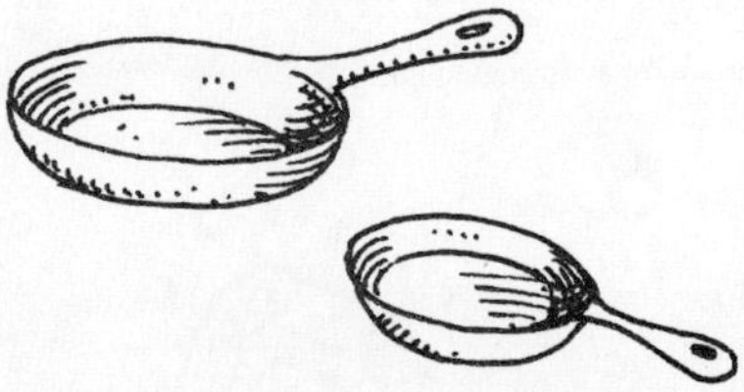

4. net 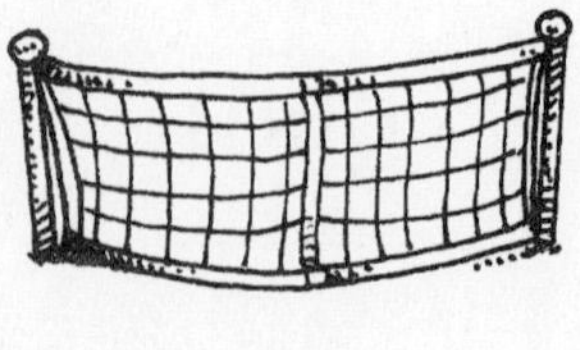

Directions: Write the number and word to tell how many.

Home Activity: Write a word that names something and have your child add *-s* to make the word mean more than one.

Name ______________________________

Write.

1. ________ 

2. ________ 

3. ________ 

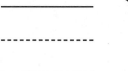

4. ________ 

5. ________ 

6. ________ 

7. ________ 

8. ________ 

9. ________ 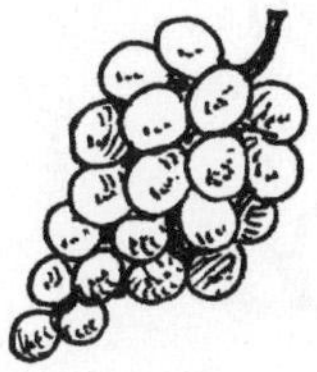

10. ________ 

Directions: Write the letters that stand for the beginning sound.

Home Activity: Ask your child to look for things in your home whose names begin with *r* blends.

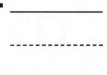

Name ____________________

Write.

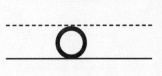

1.

_ o _

2.

_ u _

3.
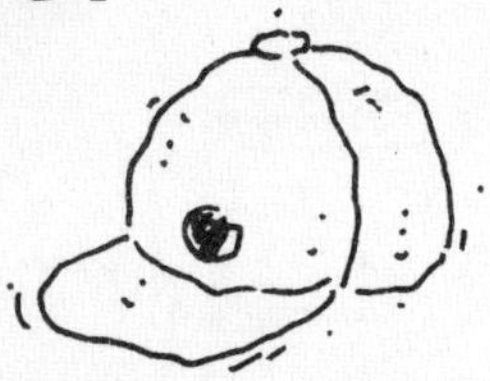
_ a _

4.

_ i _

5.

_ e _

6.
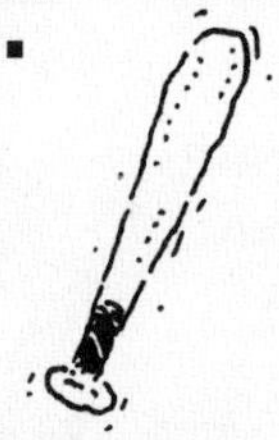
_ a _

7.

_ u _

8.

_ e _

9.

_ i _

10.

_ o _

Directions: Write the letters to complete the word.

Home Activity: Use letter cards and have your child make three-letter words.

Name ______________________________

Draw a line.

1.

st

2.

nd

3.

mp

4.

st

5.

nd

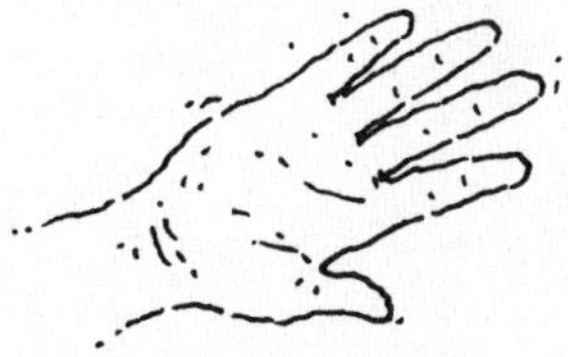

6.

nt

Directions: In each box, draw a line from a picture to the letters for its ending sound.

Home Activity: Say a picture name from the page and have your child tell if the word ends with a consonant blend.

Name ______________________________

Circle.

1.
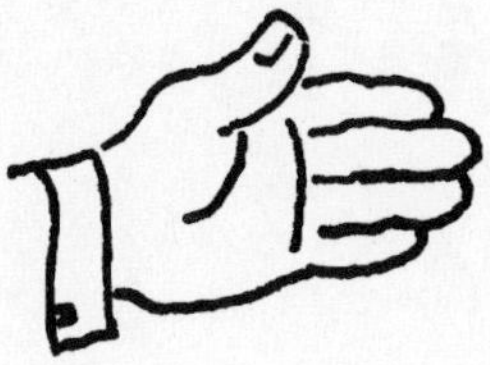
st
nd

2.

nd
mp

3.
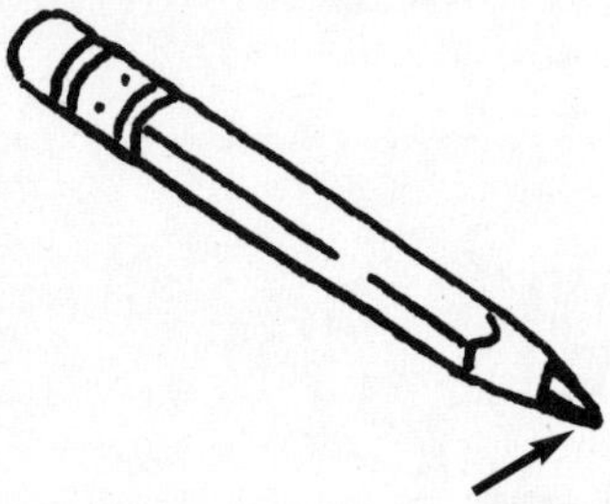
nt
mp

4.
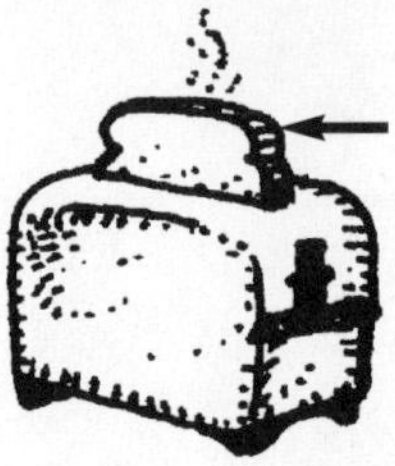
nt
st

5.

nd
nt

6.

st
nt

7.
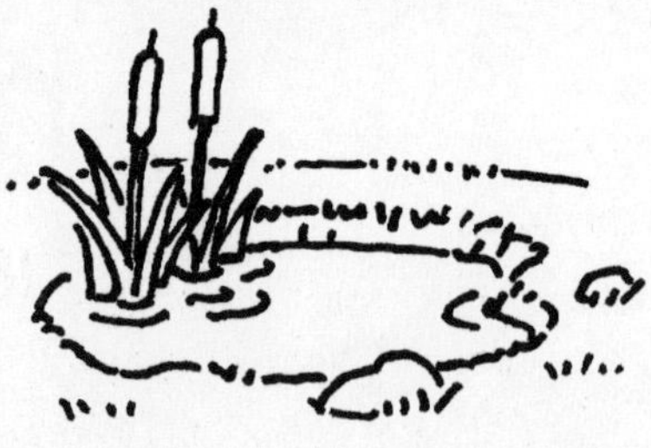
st
nd

8.

nd
mp

Directions: Name each picture. Circle the letters that stand for the ending sound.

Home Activity: Give riddle clues about a picture and have your child give the answer: *put it on a letter, small lake.*

Name ______________________________

Draw lines.

1. 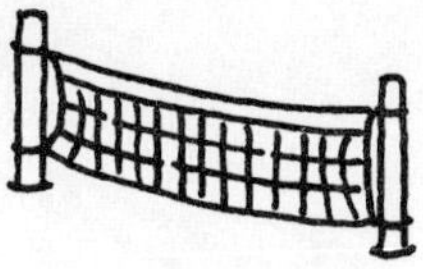 pen

2.  net

3.  jet

4. 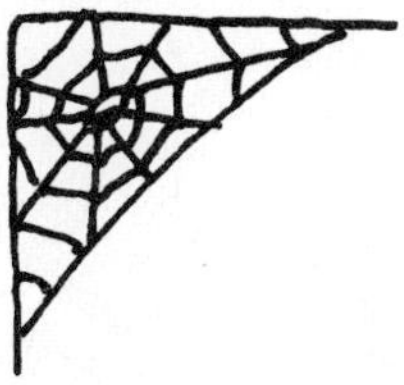 bed

5. 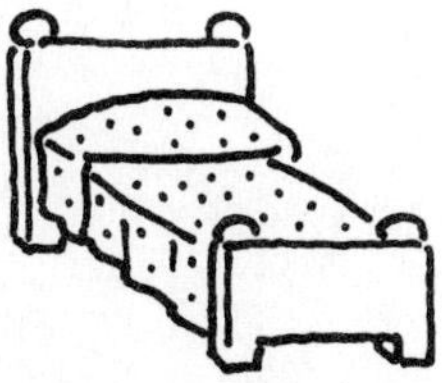 web

6.  ten

7.  well

8. 10 men

9.  bell

10. 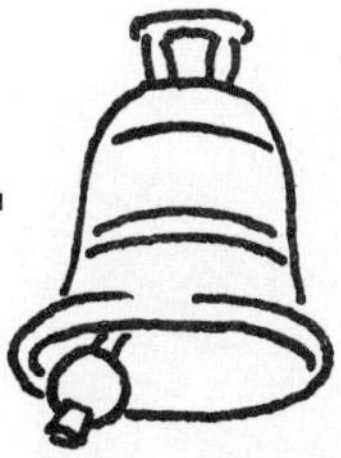 hen

Directions: Draw a line from the picture to the word that names the picture.

Home Activity: Help your child use pairs of rhyming words in sentences.

Name ______________________________

Write.

1. ________ ________ ________

2. ________ ________ ________

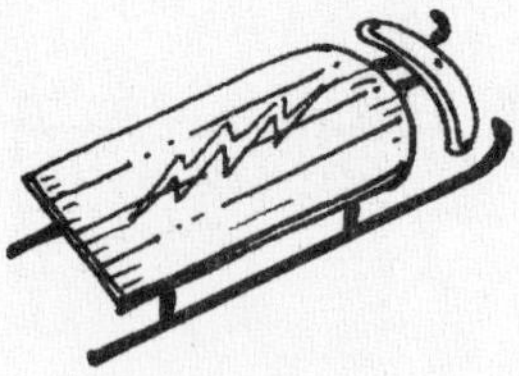

3. ________ ________ ________

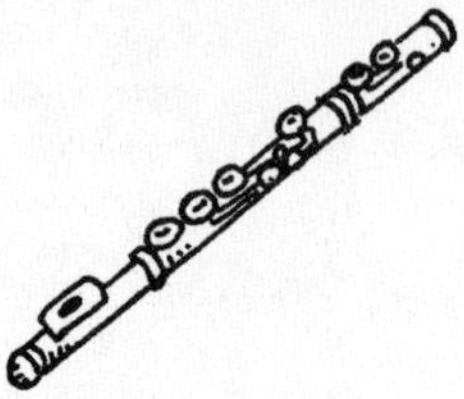

4. ________ ________ ________

5. ________ ________ ________

6. ________ ________ ________

7. ________ ________ ________

8. ________ ________ ________

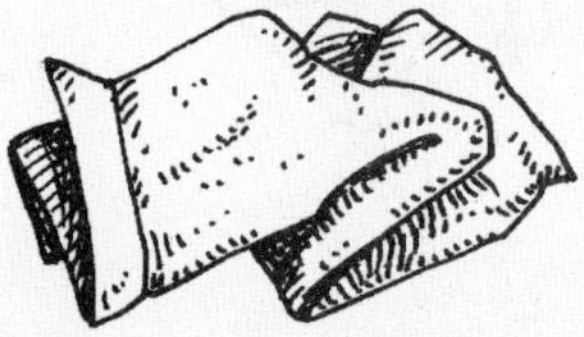

9. ________ ________ ________

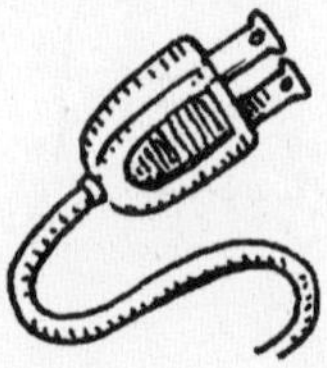

10. ________ ________ ________

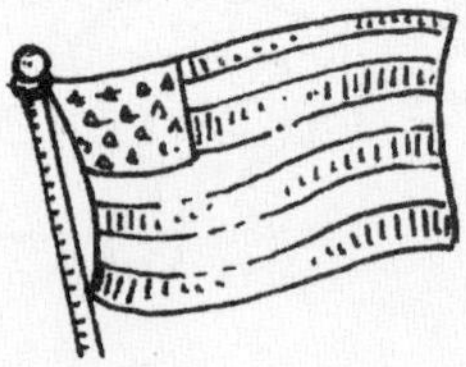

Directions: Write the letters that stand for the beginning sound.

Home Activity: Say a word. If the word begins with a blend, have your child write the letters.

Name ______________________________

Write.

1.
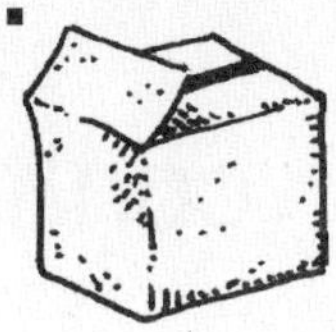
____

2.
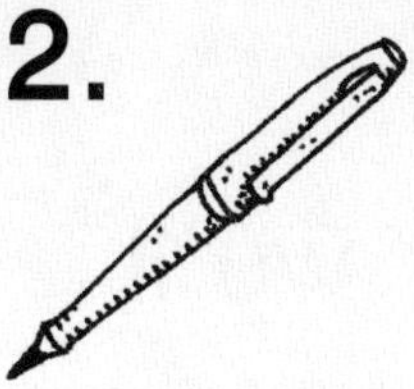
____

3.

____

4.

____

5.

____

6.

____

7.

____

8.

____

9.

____

10.

____

Directions: In each box, write the word that names the picture.

Home Activity: Write *a, e, i, o,* and *u* on paper. Help your child write three-letter words for each vowel.

Name ______________________________

Draw lines.

1.

he will	we'll
we will	she'll
she will	he'll

2.

had not	can't
were not	hadn't
can not	weren't

3.

he is	it's
she is	he's
it is	she's

4.

I will	they'll
they will	I'll
it will	it'll

5.

have not	didn't
was not	haven't
did not	wasn't

6.

does not	don't
do not	aren't
are not	doesn't

Directions: Draw lines to match the words with the contractions.

Home Activity: Have your child use the contractions in sentences.

Name ______________________

Write.

1. is + not

2. was + not

3. had + not

4. she + is

5. he + is

6. it + is

7. he + will

8. she + will

Directions: Write the contraction for the two words.

Home Activity: Say a contraction and have your child give the two words that form the contraction.

Name ______________________

Draw lines.

1.  bus

2.  sun

3.  cup

4. 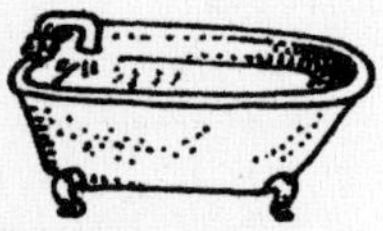 bug

5.  tub

6.  cub

7.  cut

8.  rug

9.  jug

10.  gum

Directions: Draw a line from the picture to the word that names the picture.

Home Activity: Point to a picture. Ask your child to name a rhyming word and to write the word.

Name ____________________

Write.

1.

2.

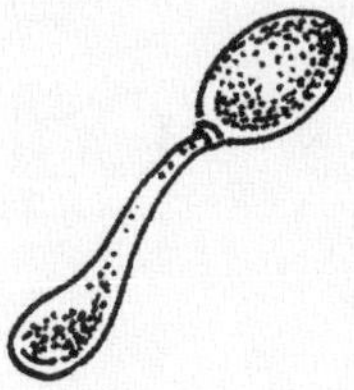

3.

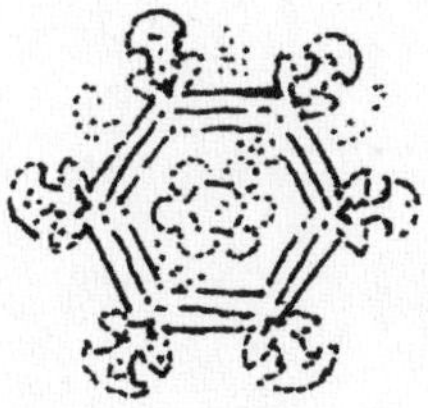

4.

5.

6.

7.

8.

9.

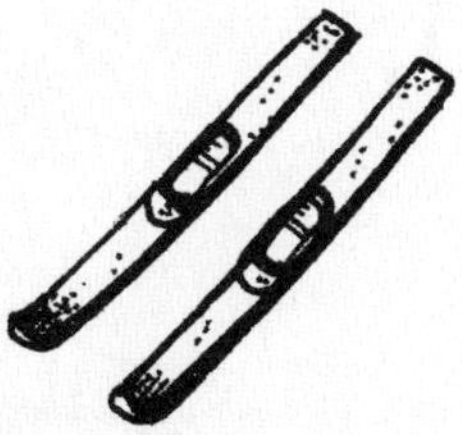

10.

Directions: Write the letters that stand for the beginning sound.

Home Activity: Point to a picture and have your child name another word that begins the same.

Name ______________________________

rake

Color.

1.

2.

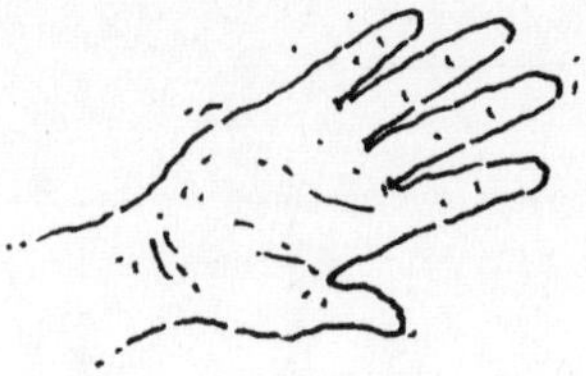

3.

4.

5.

6.

7.

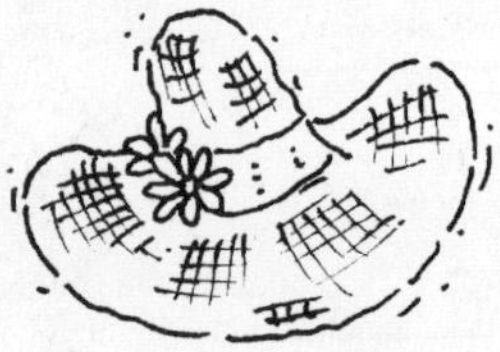

8.

9.

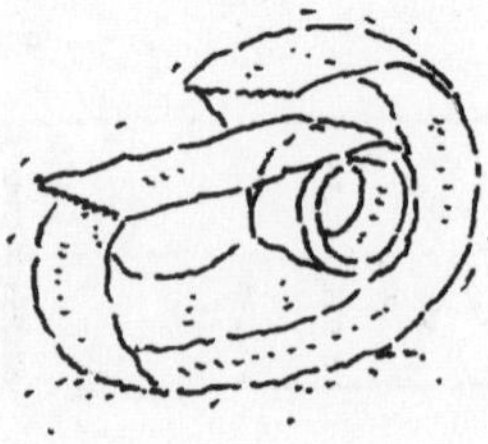

10.

Directions: Color the picture if the picture name has the same vowel sound as *rake*.

Home Activity: Make a set of short and long *a* picture cards: *can—cane.* Have your child sort the cards by vowel sound.

Name ______________________________

Write.

1. 

g_t_

2. 

c_g_

3. 

l_k_

4. 

pl_n_

5. 

sn_k_

6. 

wh_l_

Directions: Write the letters that finish each word.

Home Activity: Say two words and ask your child to tell which word has the same vowel sound as *rake*.

Name ______________________

Write.

1. want + ed

2. helps – s + ed

3. playing – ing + ed

4. packs – s + ed

5. clean + ed

6. talking – ing + ed

7. works – s + ed

8. climbing – ing + ed

9. wash + ed

10. asks – s + ed

Directions: Follow the signs to make a new word. Write the word.

Home Activity: Help your child make sentences using words from this page.

Name ________________________________

Circle.

1. 

mp st nd

2. 

nt mp nd

3. 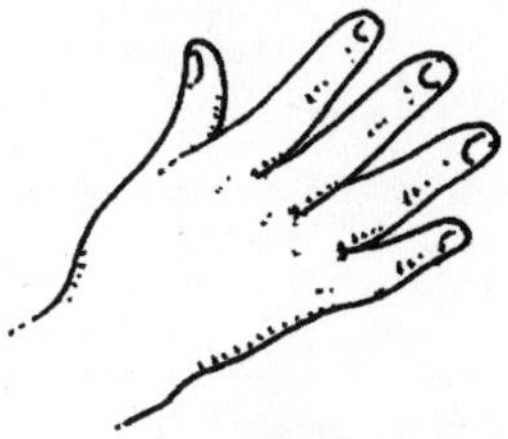

nt st nd

4. 

mp nt st

5. 

mp st nt

6. 

nt nd st

7. 

mp nd st

8. 

mp nd st

Directions: Circle the letters that stand for the ending sound.

Home Activity: Have your child make a list of words that end with *st, mp, nd,* and *nt.*

Name ______________________________

<u>g</u>ate g = /g/ 

<u>g</u>iant g = /j/ 

Circle.

1. 
g
j
game

2. 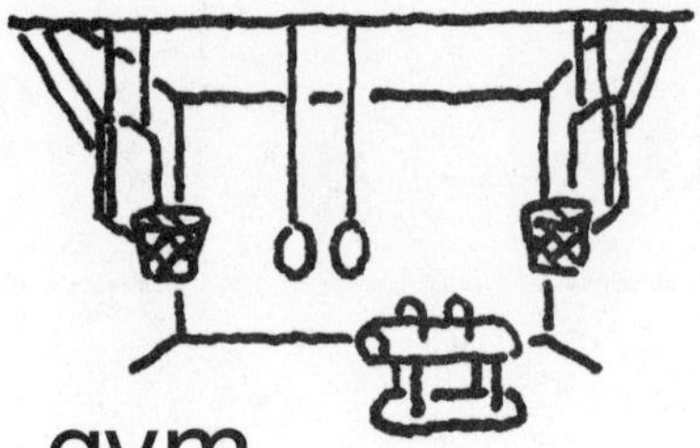
g
j
gym

3. 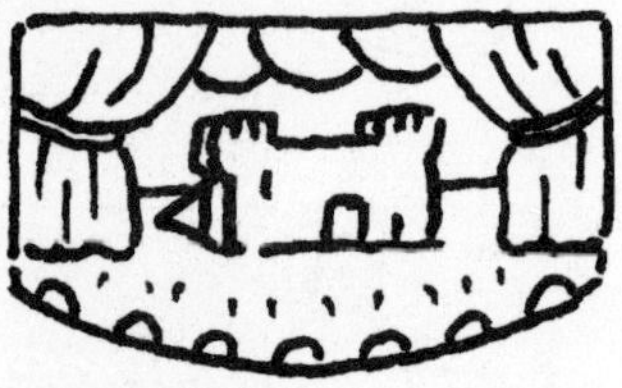
g
j
stage

4. 
g
j
wagon

5. 
g
j
giraffe

6. 
g
j
guitar

7. 
g
j
garden

8. 
g
j
page

Directions: Circle the letter that tells what sound *g* stands for in the picture name.

Home Activity: Have your child make up a tongue twister using words from the page that have the sound *g* stands for in *giant.*

Name ______________________________

lake 

Circle and write.

1.  

2.  

3.  

4.  

5.  

Directions: Circle the picture whose name has the same vowel sound as *lake.* Then write the picture name.

Home Activity: Ask your child to find things around the house that have the vowel sound in *lake.*

Name ______________________

chick

Write.

1. 

2. 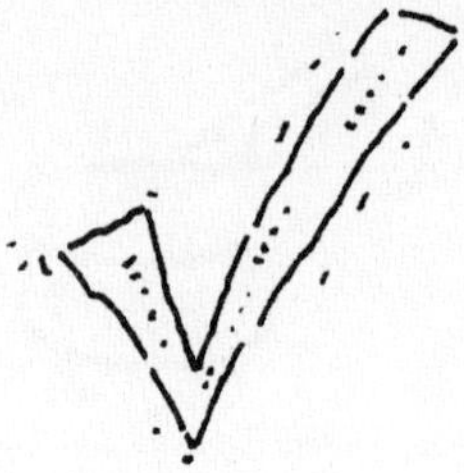

3. 

4. 

5. 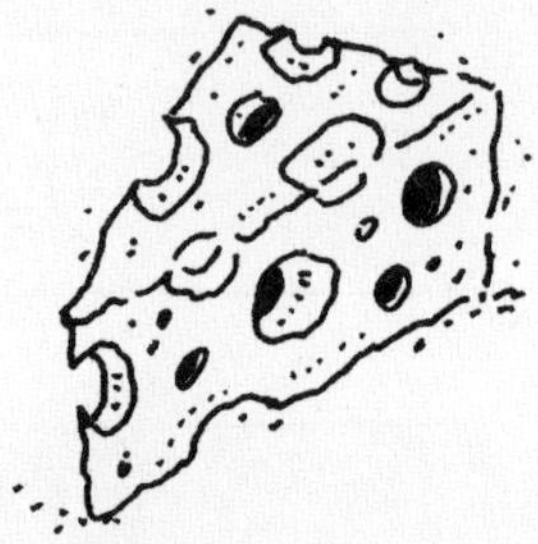

6. 

7. 

8. 

Directions: Write *ch* if the picture name begins like *chick.*

Home Activity: Have your child make sentences using words from this page that begin like *chick.*

Name ______________________________

third

Write.

1.

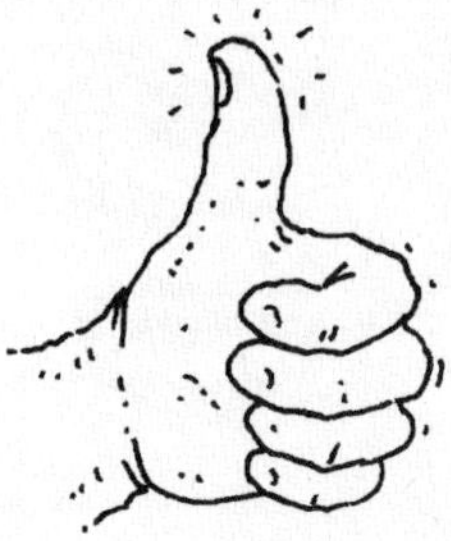

2.

3.

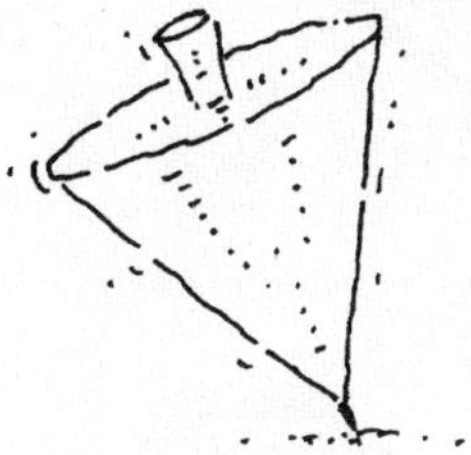

4.

5.

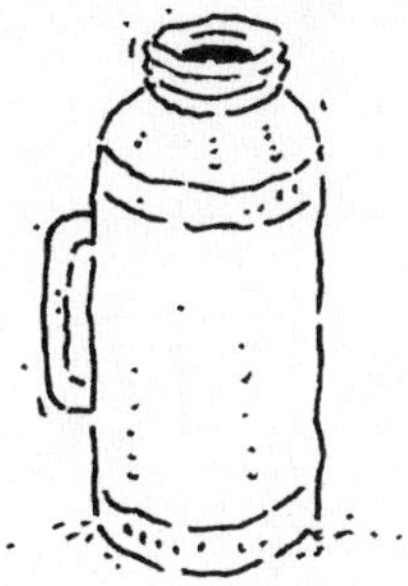

6.

7.

8.

Directions: Write *th* if the picture name begins like *third.*

Home Activity: Help your child make a list of words that begin with *th.*

Name ______________________________

Circle.

1. fr tr

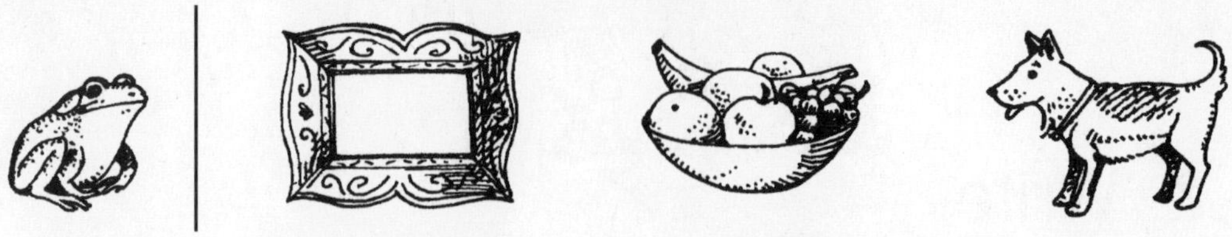

2. gr dr

3. br tr

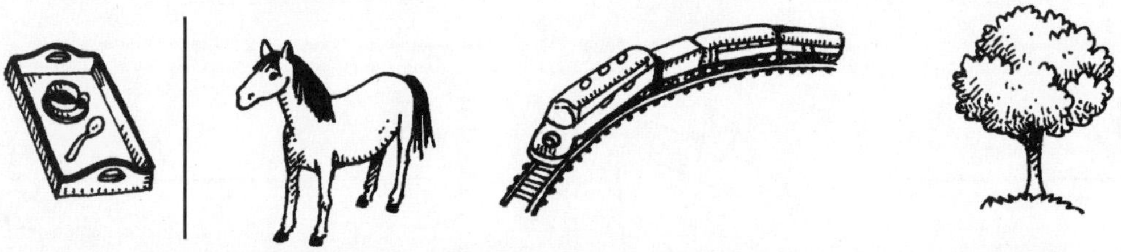

4. cl fl

5. bl gl

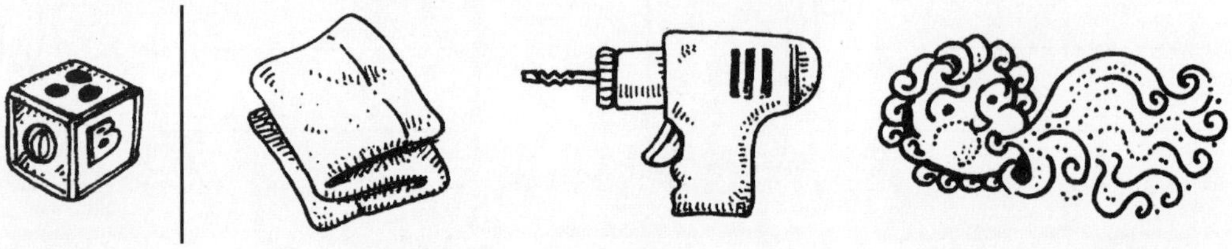

6. gl fl

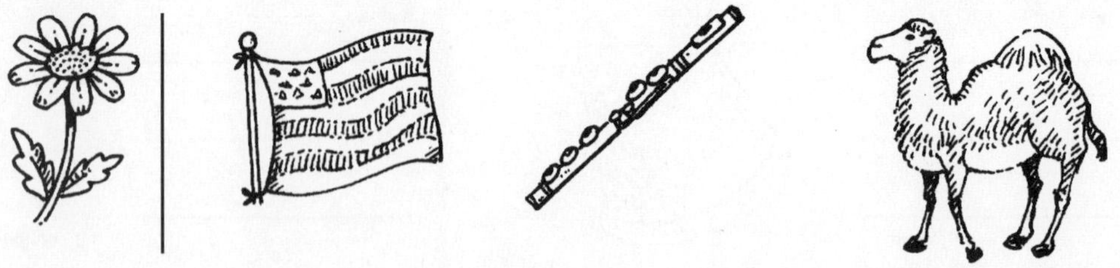

Directions: Circle the letters for the beginning sound in the first picture name. Circle the pictures that begin the same.

Home Activity: Have your child tell a story using words that begin with *r* and *l* blends.

Name ______________________

Write.

1.

2.

3.

4.

5.
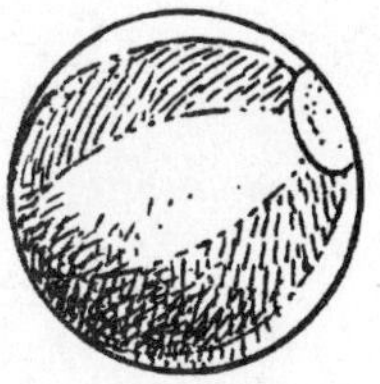

6.

7.

8.
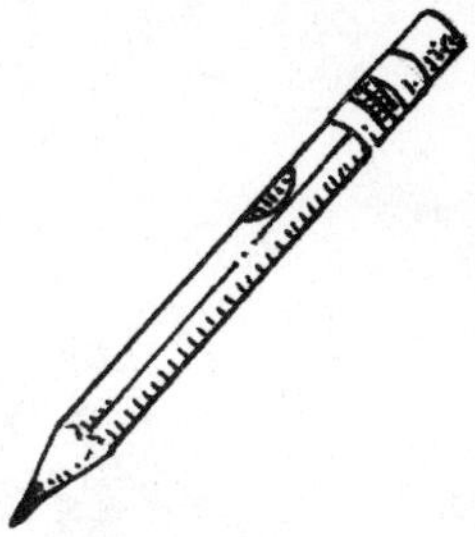

9.

10.

Directions: Write *qu* if the picture name begins like *quiet.*

Home Activity: Have your child make up a riddle about a word that begins like *quiet.*

Name ______________________________

hole

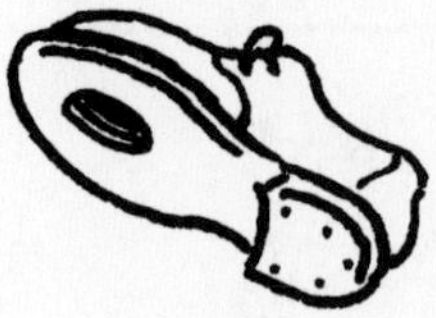

Color.

1\.

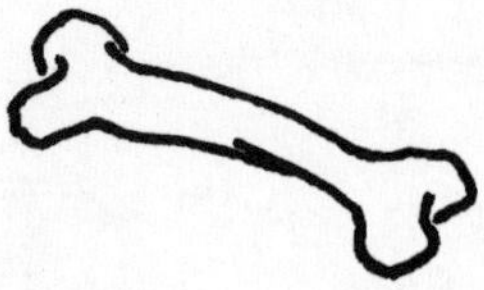

2\.

3\.

4\.

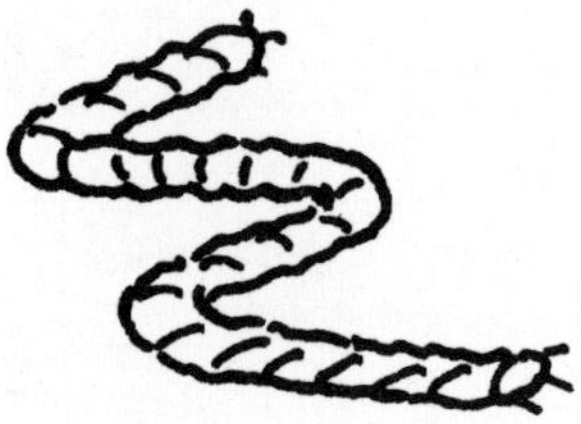

5\.

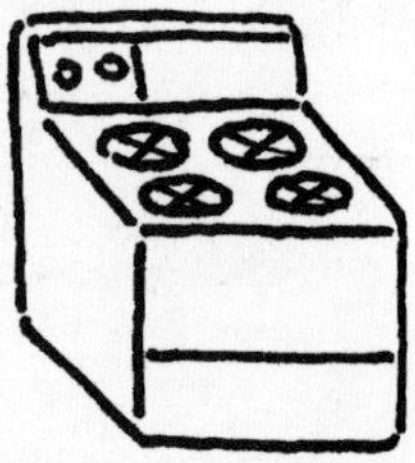

6\.

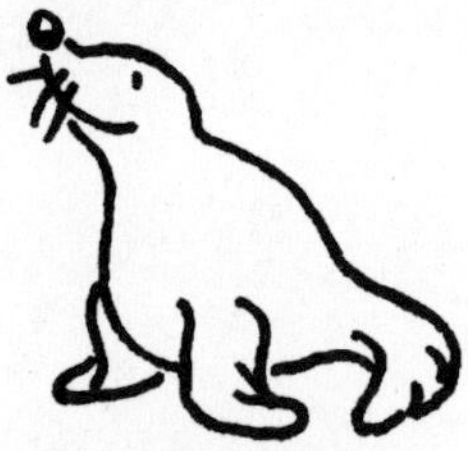

7\.

8\.

9\.

10\.

Directions: Color the picture if the picture name has the same vowel sound as *hole*.

Home Activity: Have your child draw three pictures of things that have the same vowel sound as *hole*.

Name ______________________________

Write.

1. 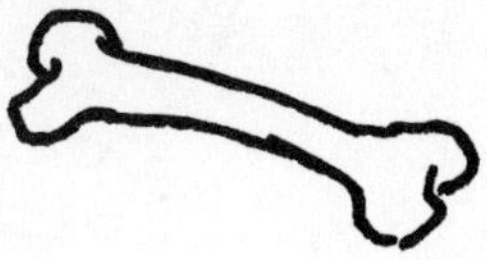

b_n_

2. 

gl_b_

3. 

r_s_

4. 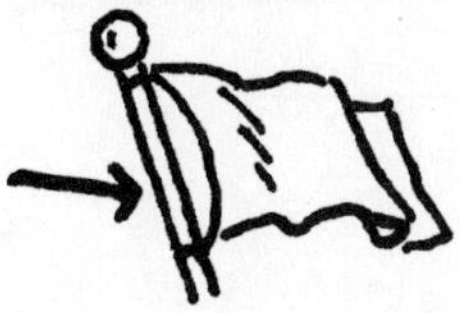

p_l_

5. 

h_m_

6. 

h_s_

7. 

n_t_

8. 

st_n_

Directions: Write the letters that finish each word.

Home Activity: Read a story and have your child listen for words with the long *o* sound in *bone.*

Name ______________________________

<u>sh</u>oe 

<u>wh</u>eel 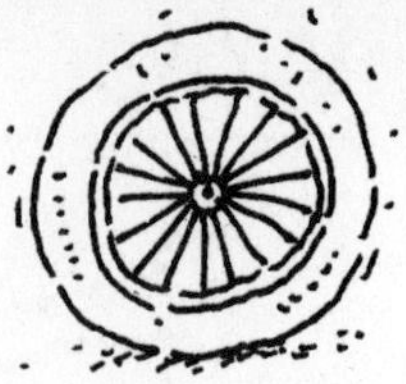

Write.

1. 

2. 

3. 

4. 

5. 

6. 

7. 

8. 

Directions: Write *sh* if the picture name begins like *shoe* and *wh* if the picture name begins like *wheel.*

Home Activity: Have your child whisper the picture names that begin with *wh* and shout the picture names that begin with *sh*.

Name ______________________

Circle and write.

1. Tom got on a ______________ .

plan plane

2. Did you ______________ bread?

bake back

3. Fish swim in the ______________ .

lack lake

4. I will ______________ the leaves.

rack rake

5. Lin wears a ______________ .

cape cap

Directions: Circle the long *a* word that completes the sentence. Then write the word.

Home Activity: Have your child name the long *a* words in this sentence: *Did the snake wear a hat to the race?*

Name ______________________________

I will play ball.
I'll

Write.

1. I hope we will go to the game.

2. I know she is playing in the park.

3. Please do not ride in the street.

4. Rob says it is a good book.

5. I think you will find your pet.

Directions: Write the contraction for the underlined words in the sentence.

Home Activity: Have your child make word cards with word pairs on one side and contractions on the other.

Name ______________________________

kite 

Color.

1. 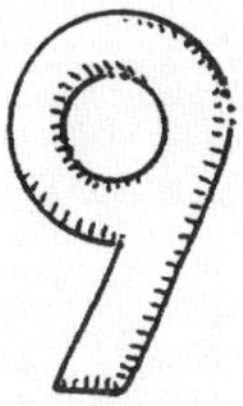

2. 

3. 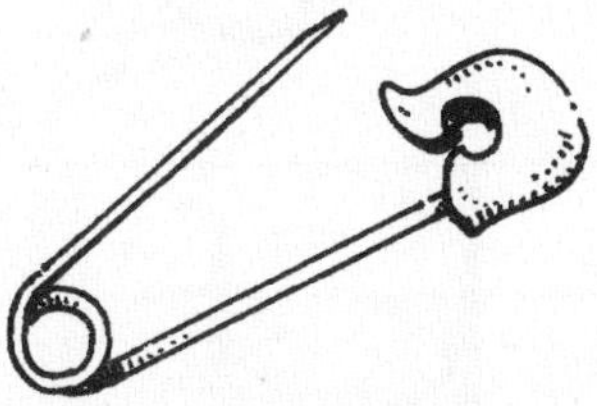

4. 

5. 

6. 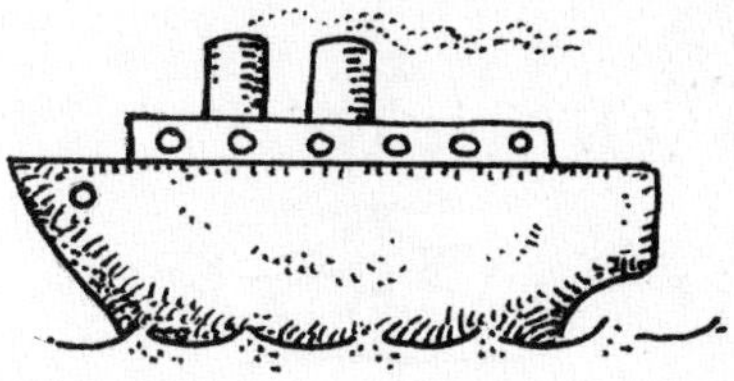

7. 

8. 

9. 

10. 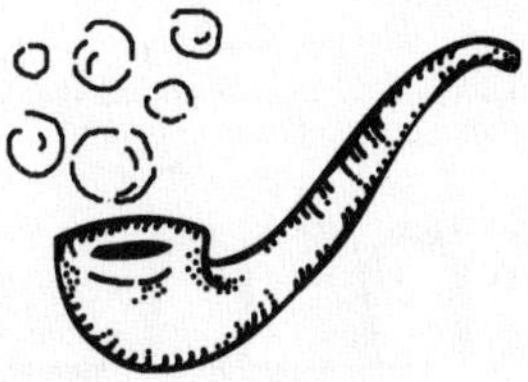

Directions: Color the picture if the picture name has the same vowel sound as *kite.*

Home Activity: Have your child make up a story about nine mice using words like *drive, smile, ride,* and *bike.*

Name ______________________________

Write.

1. 

b_k_

2. 

v_n_

3. 

br_d_

4. 

k_t_

5. 

p_n_

6. 

sm_l_

7. 

n_n_

8. 

sl_d_

Directions: Write the letters that finish each word.

Home Activity: Have your child write *smile* and draw a picture of something that makes him or her smile.

Name ______________________________

Circle.

1. 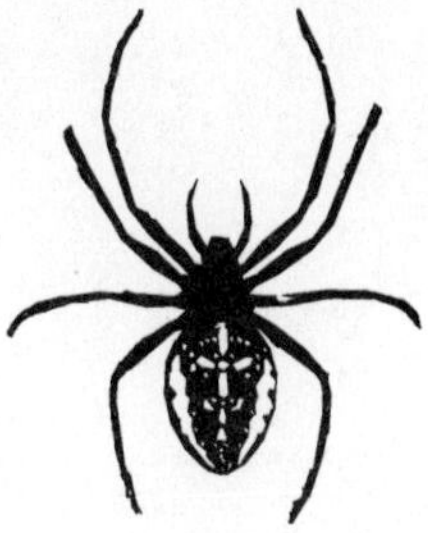

d r m

2. 

l d g

3. 

c p b

4. 

l t n

5. 

d p m

6. 

l m n

7. 

n s l

8. 

t d m

Directions: Circle the letter that stands for the sound in the middle of the picture name.

Home Activity: Give riddle clues and have your child find the picture that answers each riddle.

Name ______________________________

Circle.

1. ch wh

  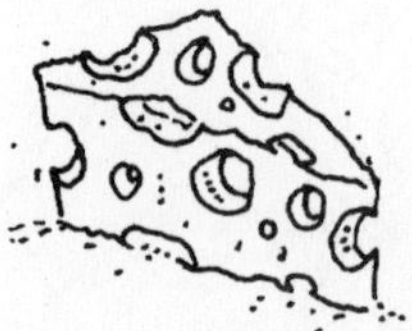 

2. wh sh

 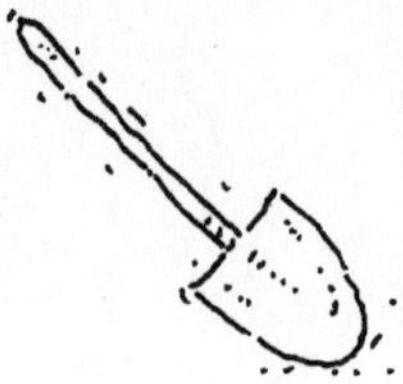 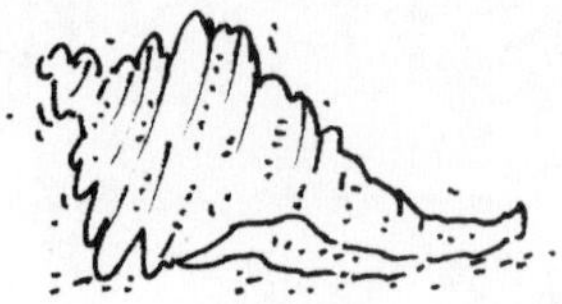 

3. th wh

4. sh wh

5. ch sh

   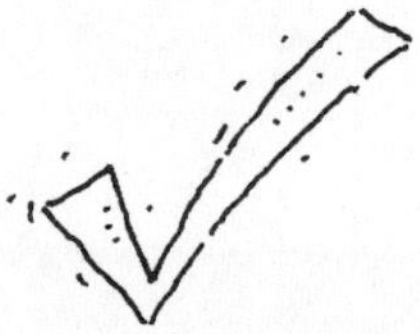

6. wh th

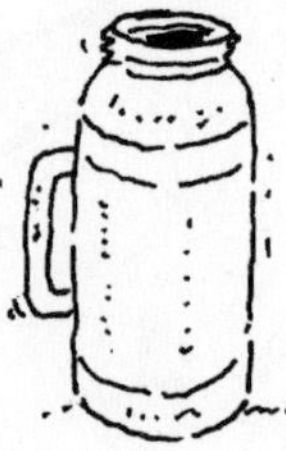 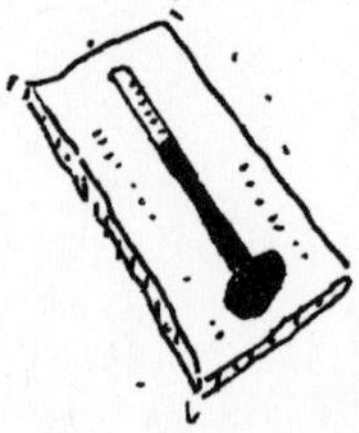  

Directions: Circle the letters for the beginning sound in the first picture name. Circle the pictures that begin the same.

Home Activity: Help your child make a list of words that begin with *ch, sh, th,* and *wh.*

Name ______________________________

cat c = /k/  mice c = /s/ 

 Circle.

1.  cent — k s

2.  race — k s

3.  city — k s

4. 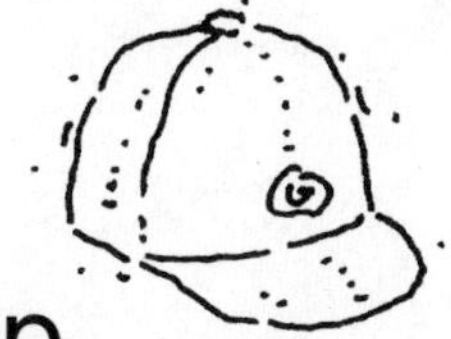 cap — k s

5.  coat — k s

6.  face — k s

7.  fence — k s

8.  cup — k s

9.  music — k s

10.  pencil — k s

Directions: Circle the letter that tells what sound *c* stands for in the picture name.

Home Activity: Say a picture name and ask your child to point to the word and tell the sound *c* stands for.

Name ______________________________

huge 

Color.

1. 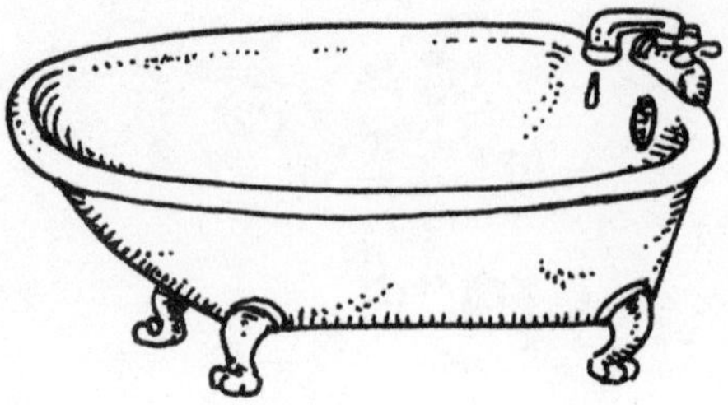

2. 

3. 

4. 

5. 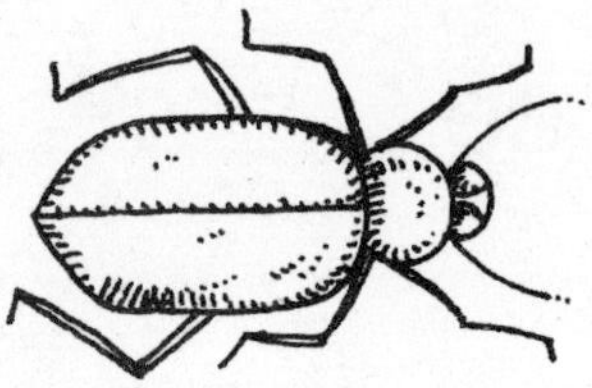

6. 

7. 

8. 

Directions: Color the picture if the picture name has the same vowel sound as *huge*.

Home Activity: Have your child write the word *cute* and draw a picture to show what the word means.

Name ______________________________

Circle.

1.

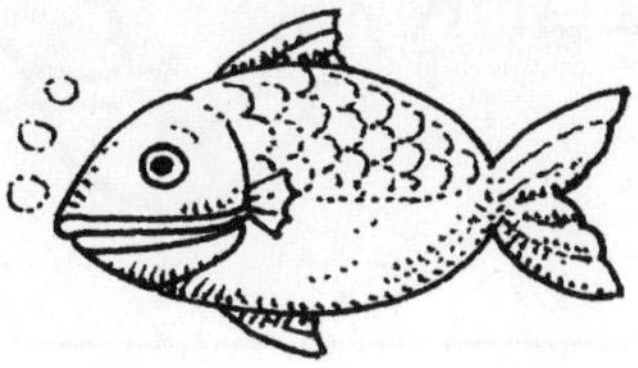

ch sh

2.

tch th

3.

th ch

4.

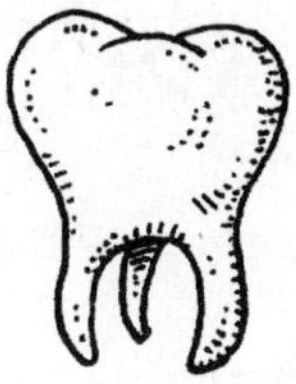

sh th

5.

ch sh

6.

sh tch

7.

tch sh

8.

th sh

Directions: Circle the letters that stand for the ending sound.

Home Activity: Have your child make a list of words that end with *ch, tch, sh,* and *th.*

Name ______________________

sing 

trunk 

Write.

1. 

2. 

3. 

4. 

5. 

6. 

7. 

8. 

Directions: Write *ng* if the picture name ends like *sing* or write *nk* if the picture name ends like *trunk*.

Home Activity: Have your child make sentences using words from this page.

Name ______________________

Circle and write.

1. I will ______________ my bike.

rid ride

2. We'll ______________ into the pool.

dive dip

3. I found a shiny ______________ .

dime dim

4. His ______________ is red.

bit bike

5. A ______________ is green.

lit lime

Directions: Circle the long *i* word that completes the sentence. Write the word.

Home Activity: Have your child draw a bike and write words that have the same vowel sound as *bike*.

Name ______________________

Circle and write.

1. I ______________ the door.

locked locking

2. She is ______________ the dog.

called calling

3. He is ______________ the house.

painting painted

4. We are ______________ a song.

sing singing

5. They ______________ to school.

walked walking

Directions: Circle the word that correctly completes the sentence. Write the word.

Home Activity: Have your child add *-ed* and *-ing* to the following words and write the new words: *sew, stay, wish, want.*

Name ______________________________

Draw lines and color.

1.

hen

he

2.

she

shed

3.

we

wet

4.

me

men

Directions: Draw lines to match the words with the pictures. Color the long *e* pictures.

Home Activity: Point to a picture and have your child spell the picture name.

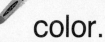

Name ______________________________

jeep

Color.

1. 

2. 

3. 

4. 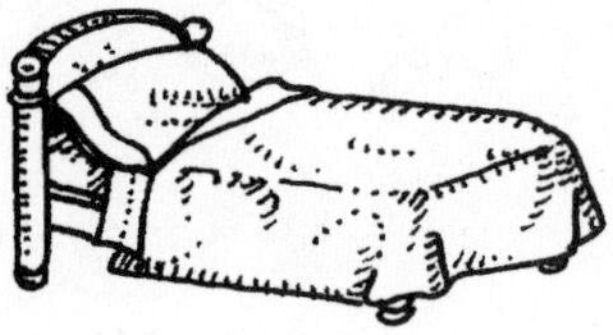

5. 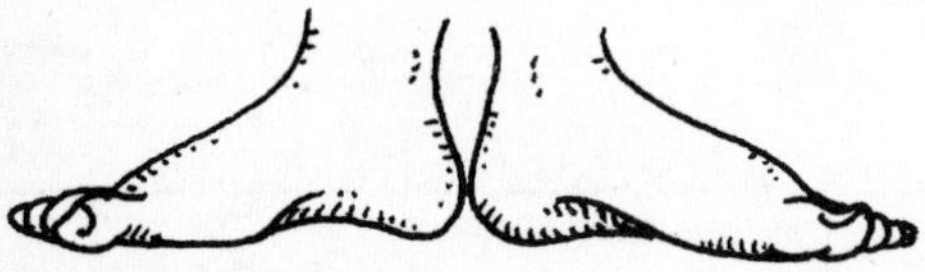

6. 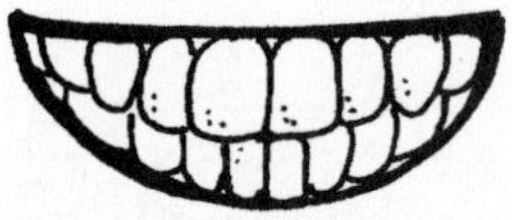

7. 

8. 

9. 

10. 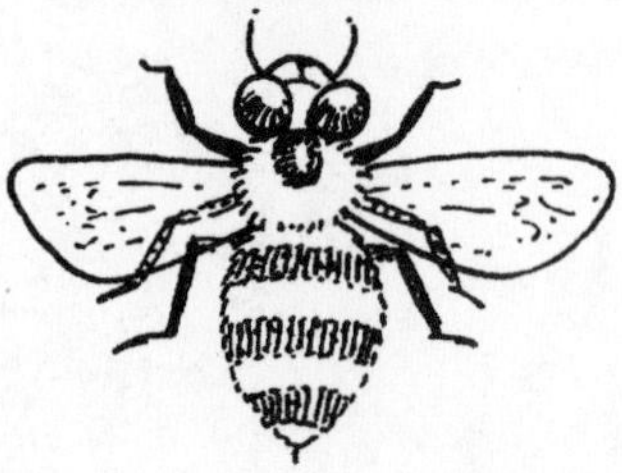

Directions: Color the picture if the picture name has the same vowel sound as *jeep*.

Home Activity: Have your child make up a rhyme using the words *bee* and *tree*.

Name ______________________________

 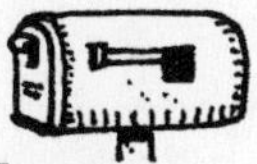

mail + box = mailbox

Write.

bee	fish	rain	sea	cook
coat	shell	hive	star	book

1.  +  = ______________________

2.  +  = ______________________

3.  +  = ______________________

4.  +  = ______________________

5.  +  = ______________________

Directions: Write the two picture names together to make a compound word.

Home Activity: Have your child make up a question about each compound word.

Name ______________________________

Write.

1. 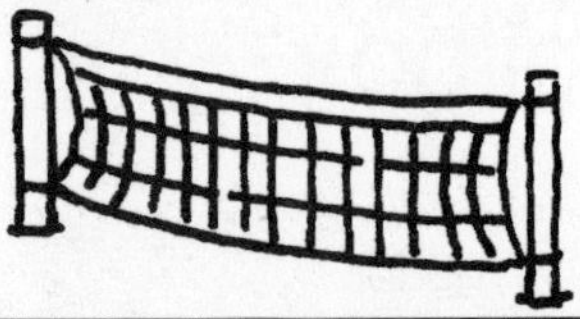

n t

2. 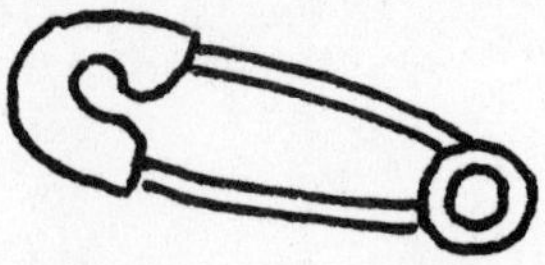

p n

3. 

b g

4. 

c t

5. 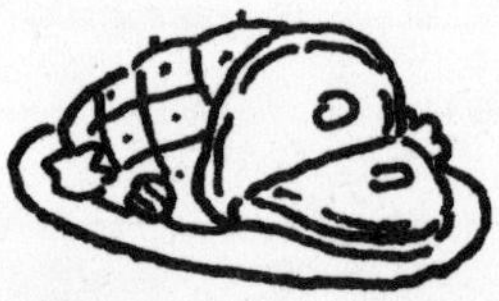

h m

6. 

s n

7. 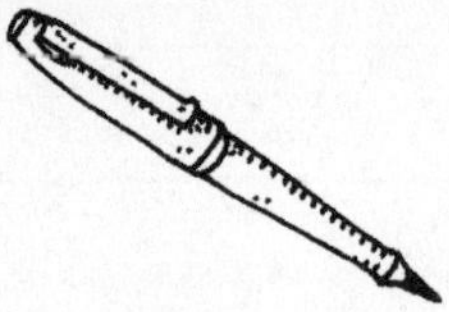

p n

8. 

p t

Directions: Write a letter to finish the picture name.

Home Activity: Have your child think of rhyming words for the words on the page.

Name ______________________

Circle.

1. 

d t s

2. 

s n b

3. 

m g c

4. 

c n p

5. 

g f l

6. 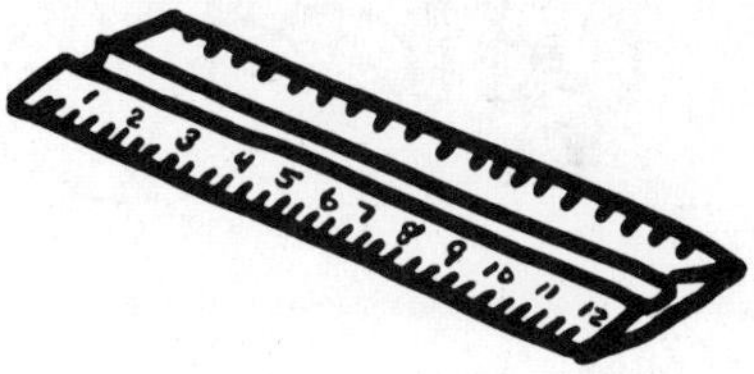

t m l

7. 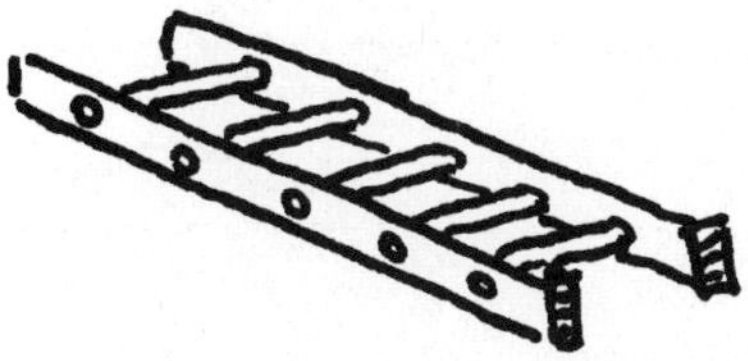

b f d

8. 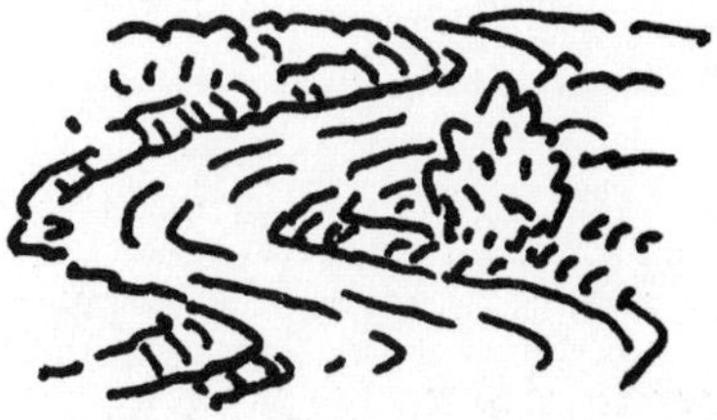

s v k

Directions: Circle the letter that stands for the middle sound in the picture name.

Home Activity: Say other words and ask your child to name the letter that stands for the middle sound.

Name ____________________

bean

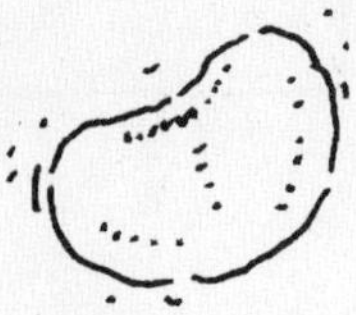

Color.

1.

2.

3.

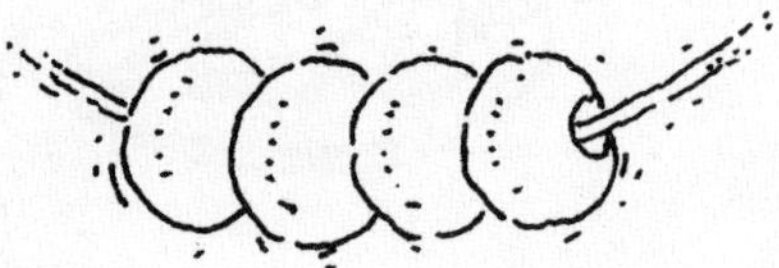

4.

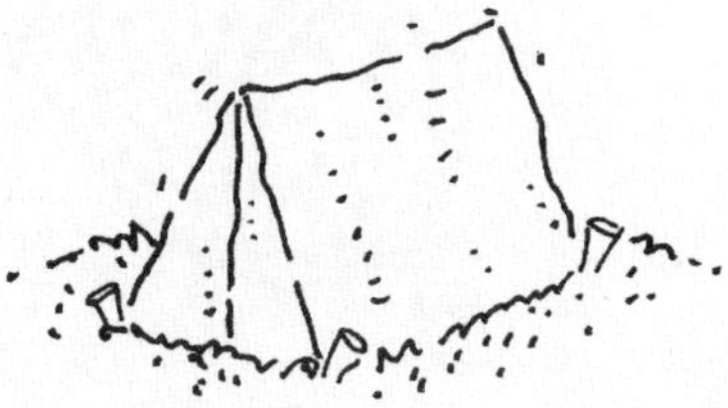

5.

6.

7.

8.

9.

10.

Directions: Color the picture if the picture name has the same vowel sound as *bean.*

Home Activity: Read a story and ask your child to listen for long *e* words.

Name ______________________

Write.

1. 

l__f

2. 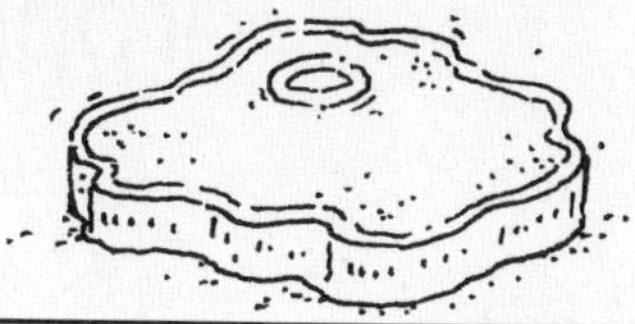

m__t

3. 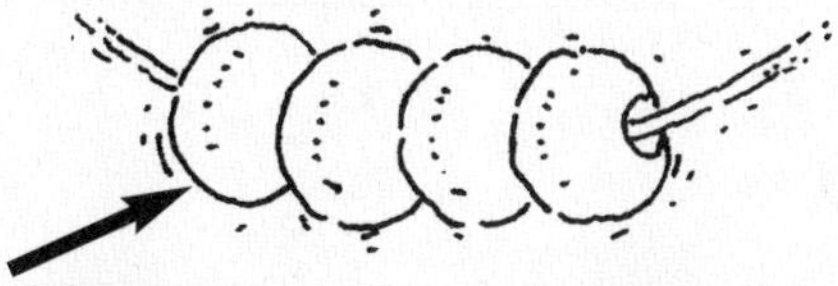

b__d

4. 

wr__th

5. 

p__ch

6. 

t__m

7. 

b__ch

8. 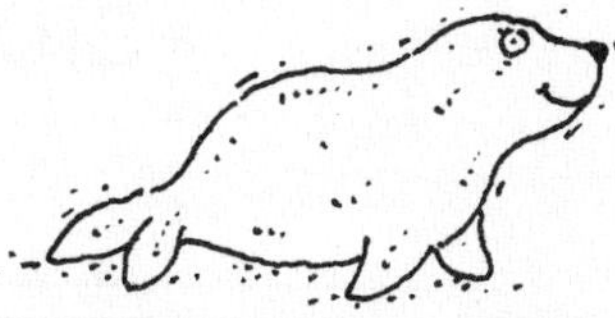

s__l

Directions: Write the letters to finish each word.

Home Activity: Point to a word and have your child use it in a sentence.

Name ______________________

dropped

Write.

1. The bunny ______________ fast.
hop

2. We ______________ for the team.
clap

3. I ______________ at the park.
stop

4. Ana ______________ her pet.
hug

Directions: Add *-ed* to the word. Write the new word to finish the sentence.

Home Activity: Ask your child to write a sentence for each word.

Name ______________________________

Circle and write.

1. A ______________ was in the box.

robe   rob

2. I wrote a ______________.

not   note

3. We ______________ the bus.

rod   rode

4. The dog had a ______________.

box   bone

5. This is my ______________.

hop   home

Directions: Circle the long *o* word that completes the sentence. Then write the word.

Home Activity: Have your child look through magazines or newspapers for other words that have the vowel sound in *bone*.

Name ______________________________

Write.

1. 

a pot for tea

____

2. 

a brush for paint

____

3. 

a shell from the sea

____

4. 

a room for a bed

____

5. 

a house for a bird

____

Directions: Use the clue to write a compound word.

Home Activity: Help your child look for compound words in newspapers and magazines. Make a list of the words.

Name ______________________

Draw lines and circle.

1.  paint

2.  hat

3.  pan

4.  rain

5.  sail

6.  train

7.  pail

8.  flag

9.  cap

10. 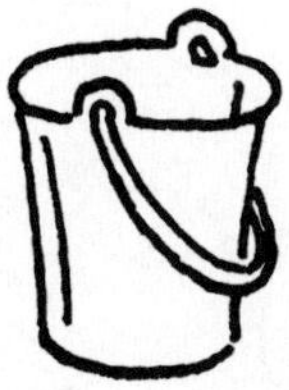 snail

Directions: Draw a line from the picture to the word that names the picture. Circle the words with the long *a* sound.

Home Activity: Have your child make up a rhyme using words from the page.

Name ______________________

say

Circle and write.

1. 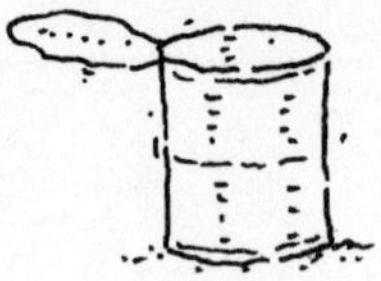 can  clay

2. 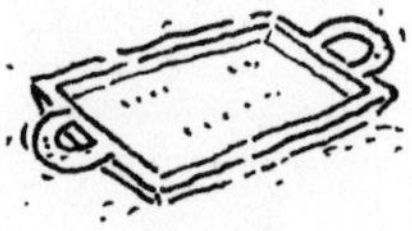 tray  trap

3.  ran  ray

4.  jam  jay

5.  play 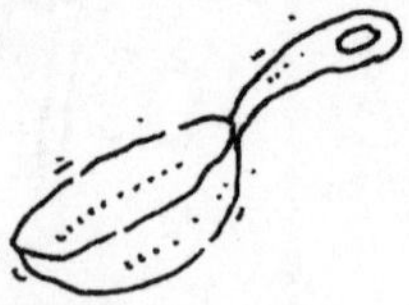 pan

Directions: Circle the picture whose name is spelled like *say.* Write the picture name.

Home Activity: Help your child look for long *a* words in a storybook.

Name ______________________

I am at home.
I'm

Write.

1. I will read a book. ______________

2. I am a big sister. ______________

3. I did not find my book. ______________

4. He is my friend. ______________

5. She is a good player. ______________

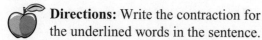

Directions: Write the contraction for the underlined words in the sentence.

Home Activity: Have your child look for contractions in a newspaper and tell what words each contraction stands for.

Name ______________________________

Circle and write.

1. 
bake
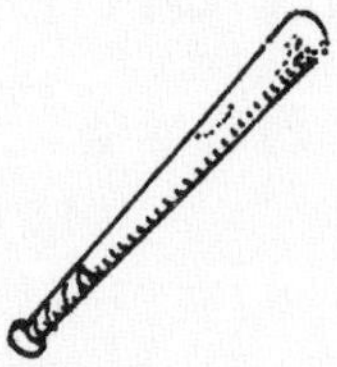 

2. 
bike
 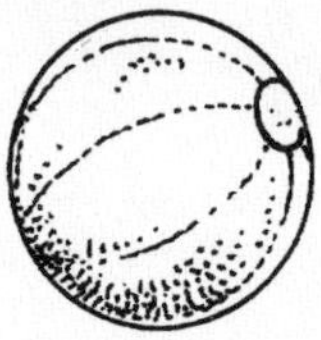

3. 
hose
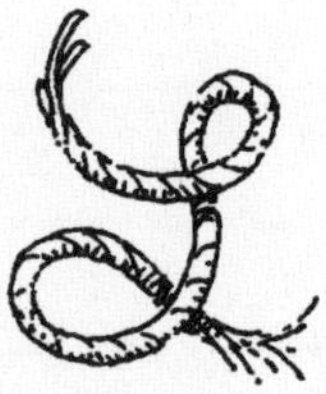 

4. 
mule
 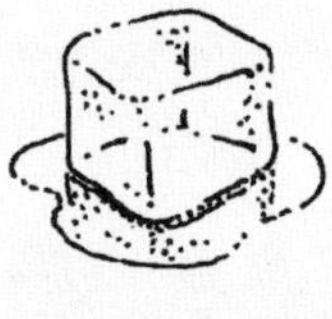

5. 
pine
 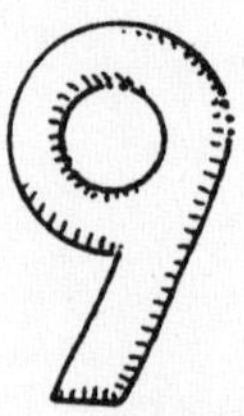

Directions: In each row, circle the picture whose name has the same vowel sound as the word and write the picture name.

Home Activity: Help your child make a list of long vowel words.

Name ______________________________

Draw lines.

1.

wh 

sh 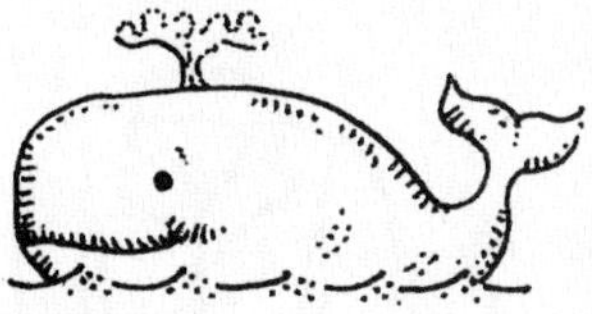

2.

sh 

th 

3.

th 

ch 

4.

ch 

wh 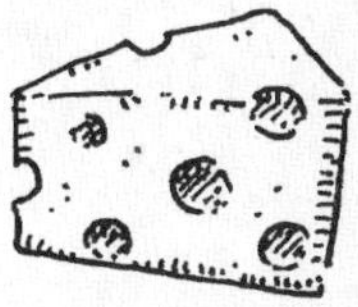

5.

wh 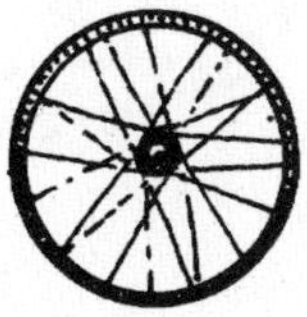

sh 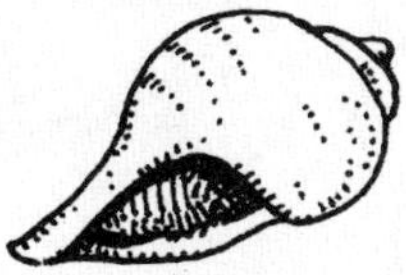

6.

sh 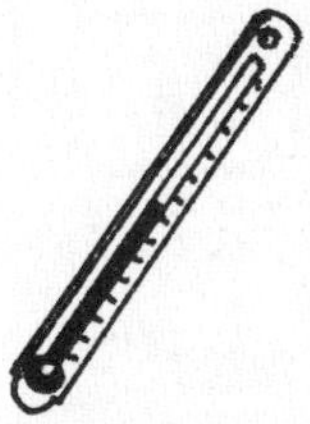

th 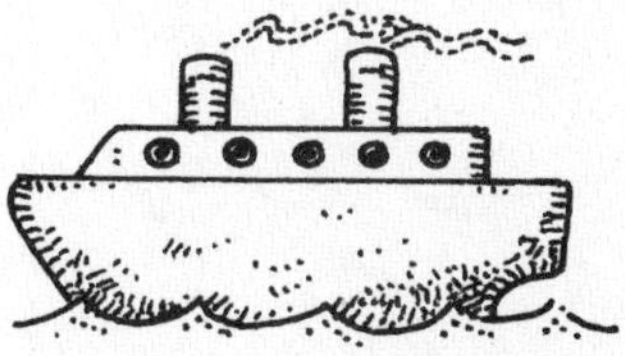

Directions: In each box, draw a line from the picture to the letters for the beginning sound.

Home Activity: Have your child make up sentences using the *ch, sh, th,* and *wh* words on this page.

Name ______________________

Draw lines and circle.

1.  goat

2.  boat

3.  soap

4. 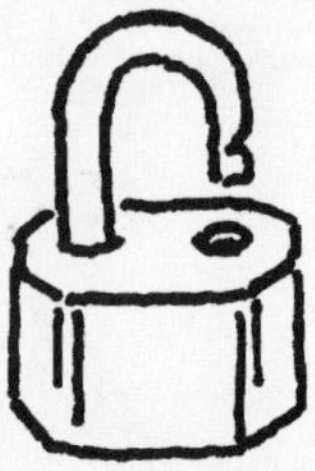 road

5.  lock

6.  coat

7.  toast

8.  socks

9. 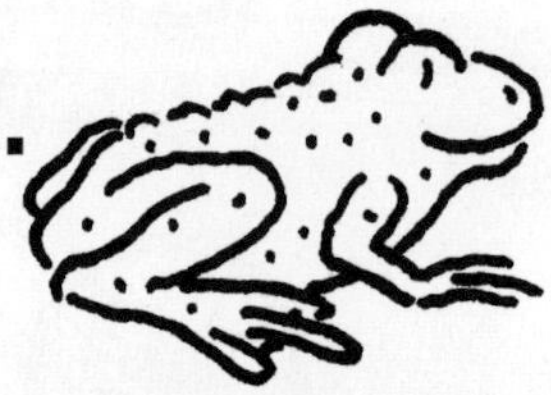 fox

10.  toad

Directions: Draw a line from the picture to the word that names the picture. Circle the words with the long *o* sound.

Home Activity: Have your child make up a poem using the words *goat, coat, boat,* and *float.*

Name ____________________

Draw lines and circle.

1.  mop

2. 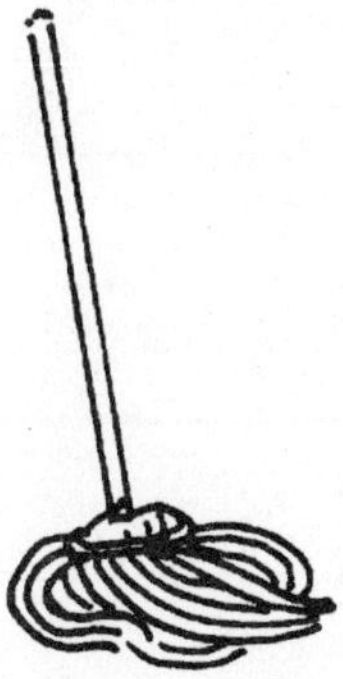 bowl

3.  cot

4.  arrow

5.  pillow

6.  clock

7.  blow

8.  box

9.  bow

10.  mow

Directions: Draw a line from the picture to the word that names the picture. Circle the words with the long *o* sound.

Home Activity: Have your child choose a word from this page and write a sentence using the word.

Name ______________________________

bat + ing = batting

Write.

1. tap + ing

2. run + ing

3. tip + ing

4. cut + ing

5. hug + ing

6. set + ing

7. stop + ing

8. rub + ing

Directions: Follow the signs to make a new word. Write the word.

Home Activity: Help your child make sentences using words from this page.

Name ______________________

Circle and write.

1.

we

bed

he

2.
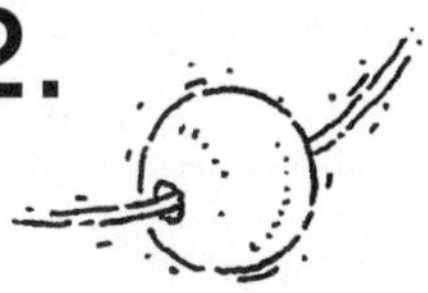
bead
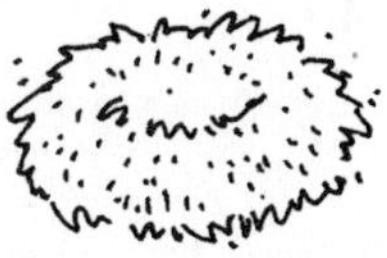
nest

read

3.

meal

ten

seal

4.

three

tree

tent

5.

sheep

jeep

hen

Directions: Circle the picture whose name rhymes with the first word and write the picture name.

Home Activity: Help your child make a list of the long *e* words on the page.

Name ______________________________

Circle.

1.

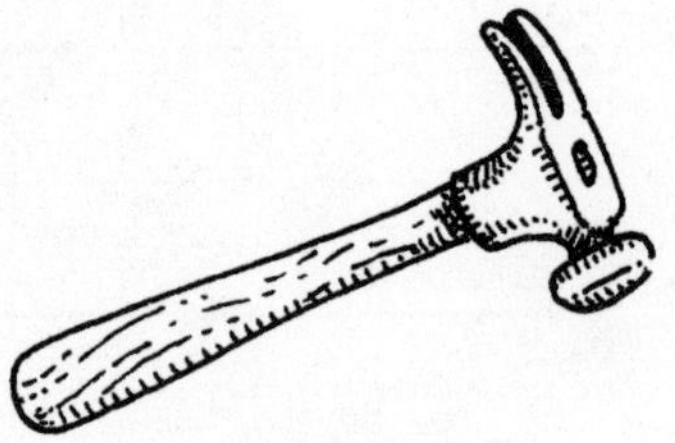

d m r

2.

n p g

3.

l c b

4.

d b h

5.

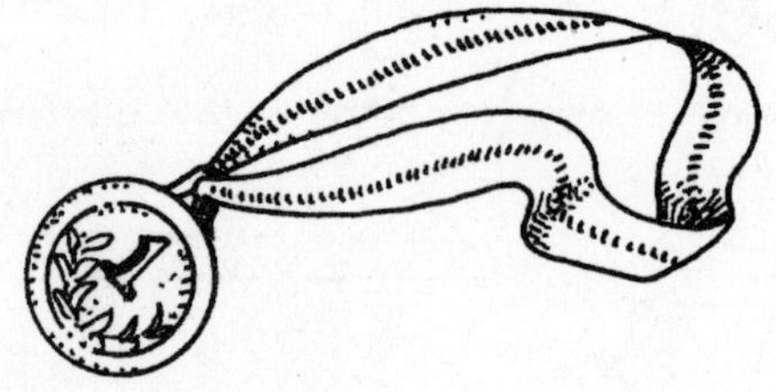

n f d

6.

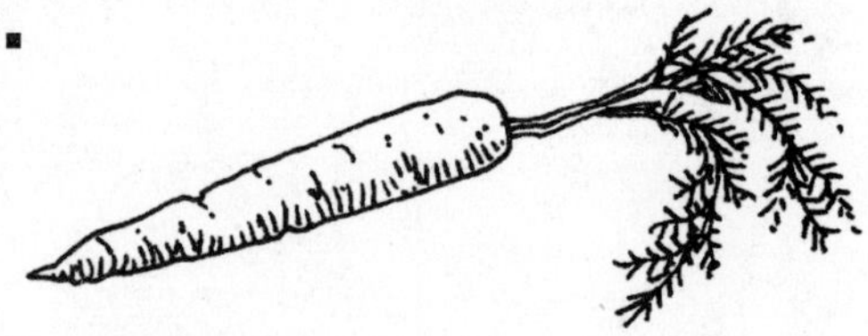

r d p

7.

s l p

8.

d n l

Directions: Circle the letter for the middle sound in each picture name.

Home Activity: Help your child write other words with one or two consonants in the middle.

Name ______________________________

dried 

Draw lines and circle.

1.  tie
2.  pig
3.  pie
4.  bib
5.  cried
6.  fish
7.  untie
8.  six
9.  lie
10.  fried

Directions: Draw a line from the picture to the word that names the picture. Circle the words with the long *i* sound.

Home Activity: Have your child use the long *i* words in sentences.

Name ______________________

high 

Draw lines and circle.

1.  right

2.  light

3. 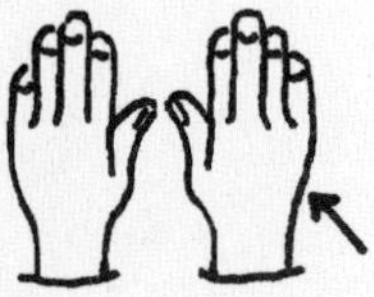 list

4. 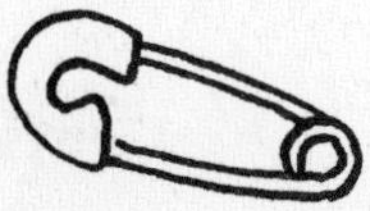 flight

5.  pin

6.  sight

7.  sink

8.  night

9.  stick

10.  bright

Directions: Draw a line from the picture to the word that names the picture. Circle the words with the long *i* sound.

Home Activity: Have your child make up a rhyme using words from the page.

Name ______________________________

the boy's hat

Write.

1. hat for a girl

the ______________ hat

2. bone for a dog

a ______________ bone

3. milk for the cat

the ______________ milk

4. book for Tom

______________ book

Directions: Write the word that shows who the item belongs to.

Home Activity: Point to items and have your child use a word with *'s* to tell who owns the item.

Name ______________________________

Circle and write.

1. 
rain

2. 
jay

 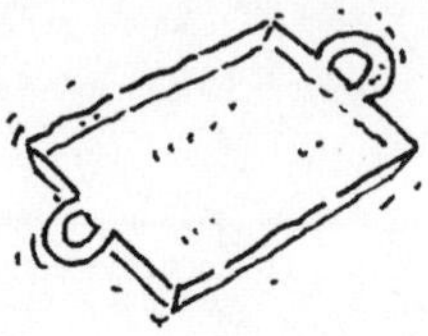

3. 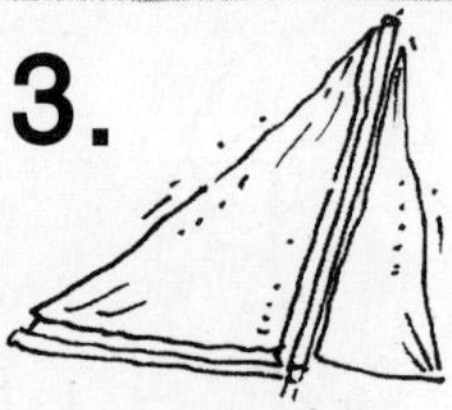
sail

4. 
clay

5. 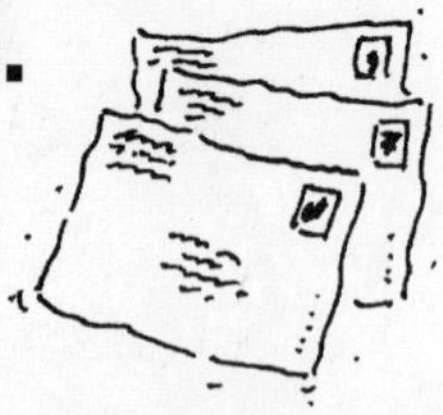
mail

 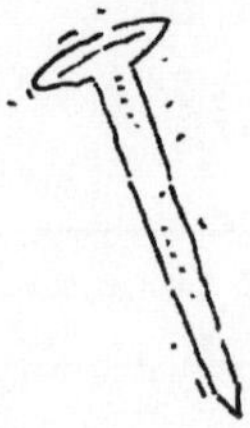

Directions: Circle the picture whose name rhymes. Write the picture name. Underline the letters that spell long *a*.

Home Activity: Help your child make a list of long *a* words.

Name ____________________

Draw lines.

1.

it is	let's
let us	here's
here is	it's

2.

who is	who's
she is	she's
what is	what's

3.

has not	doesn't
must not	hasn't
does not	mustn't

4.

was not	didn't
were not	weren't
did not	wasn't

5.

is not	don't
are not	aren't
do not	isn't

6.

that is	I'm
there is	that's
I am	there's

Directions: Draw lines to match the words with their contractions.

Home Activity: Have your child use the contractions in sentences.

Name ______________________________

spy

Color.

1.

2.

3.

4.

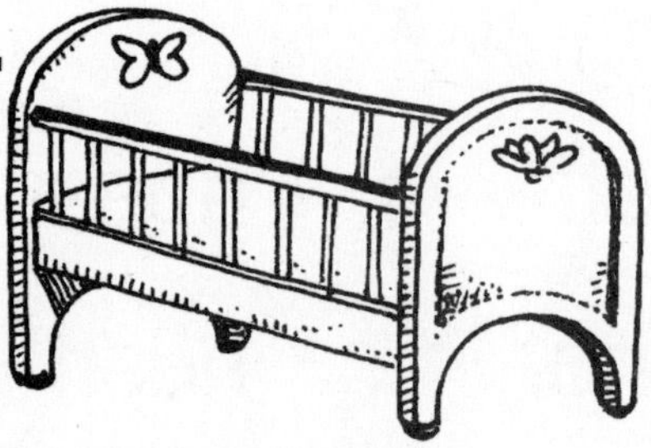

5.

6.

7.

8.

Directions: Color the picture if the picture name has the same vowel sound as *spy.*

Home Activity: Look in magazines for pictures or words that have a long *i* sound.

Name ______________________________

cloudy 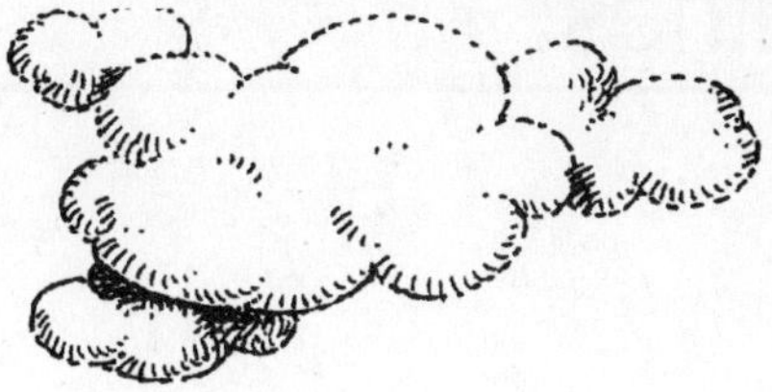

Color.

1. 

2. 

3. 

4. 

5. 

6. 

7. 

8. 

Directions: Color the picture if the picture name has the same ending vowel sound as *cloudy.*

Home Activity: Help your child think of animal names that end with long *e* *(bunny, pony, puppy).*

Name ______________________

Draw lines.

1.

rain fish

star ball

base bow

2.

sail coat

cook boat

rain book

Directions: Draw lines to match the words that make compound words.

Home Activity: Have your child use the compound words in sentences.

Name ______________________

Circle and write.

1.

pie

tree

tie

2.

light

night

tire

3.

fight

hay
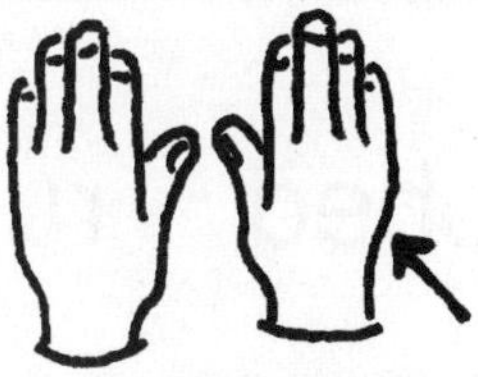
right

4.

dried

gate

cried

5.

tried

fried

nail

Directions: Circle the picture whose name rhymes with the first word and write the picture name.

Home Activity: Help your child make a list of long *i* words.

Name ______________________

Circle and write.

1. I ______________ my pet.

hugged hugging

2. He was ______________ his leg.

rubbed rubbing

3. The dog ______________ its tail.

wagged wagging

4. We ______________ on the rope.

tugged tugging

Directions: Circle the word that correctly completes the sentence. Write the word.

Home Activity: Have your child use one of the *-ed* or *-ing* words in a sentence.

Name ______________________

glue

Write.

1. This story is ______________.

tub true

2. Clint gave us a ______________.

clue cub

3. The sky is ______________.

bug blue

4. Her name is ______________.

Sue Saw

Directions: Write the word that correctly completes the sentence. Then underline the letters that stand for the vowel sound.

Home Activity: Point to a word and have your child name the letters that stand for the vowel sound.

Name ______________________________

drew

Draw lines.

1.

threw

three

chew

2.

grew

blew

block

3.

flew

note

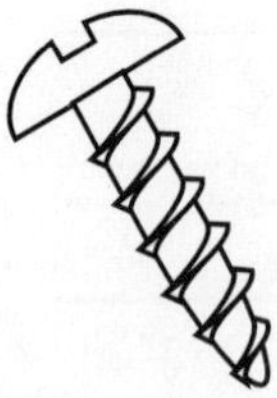

screw

4.

stop

stew

crew

Directions: Draw lines from the words to the pictures that the words name.

Home Activity: Have your child write two rhyming words with *ew*.

Name ______________________

Write.

box boxes

1. I see a ______________ .

2. I see two ______________ .

3. Lon ______________ in gym class.

wish wishes

4. I made three ______________ .

5. Pat ______________ she had a pet.

6. I made a ______________ .

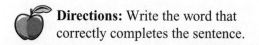

Directions: Write the word that correctly completes the sentence.

Home Activity: Have your child add *-es* to make words that mean more than one.

Name ______________________________

Circle and write.

1.  baby |  cry  lady

2.  dry |  fly  bunny

3.  twenty |  penny  fry

4.  sky |  sixty  spy

5.  pony |  try  jelly

Directions: Circle the picture with the same final vowel sound as the first word and write the picture name.

Home Activity: Point to a word. Have your child read the word and tell what vowel sound *y* stands for.

Name ______________________

Circle.

1.

nk ng

2.

nk ng

3.

nk ng

4.

nk ng

5.

nk ng

6.

nk ng

7.

nk ng

8.

nk ng

Directions: Circle the letters that stand for the ending sound in each picture name.

Home Activity: Point to a picture and ask your child to name words that rhyme with the picture name.

Name ______________________________

f<u>ar</u>m 

Color.

1. 

2. 

3. 

4. 

5. 

6. 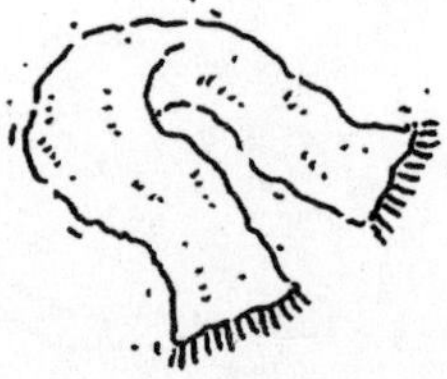

7. 

8. 

9. 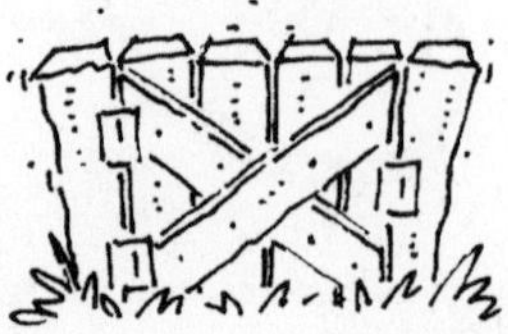

10. 

Directions: Color the picture if the picture name has the same vowel sound as *farm.*

Home Activity: Point to a picture and help your child write the picture name.

Name ____________________________________

Write.

1. 

c _ _ d

2. 

b _ _ n

3. 

st _ _

4. 

f _ _ m

5. 

y _ _ n

6. 

c _ _

7. 

p _ _ k

8. 

j _ _

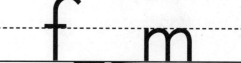

Directions: Write the letters that finish each word.

Home Activity: Scramble one of the words and let your child rearrange the letters to make a word—*nray (yarn).*

Name ______________________

glad + ly   gladly

Write.

1.  slow + ly ______________

2.  soft + ly ______________

3.  warm + ly ______________

4.  deep + ly ______________

5.  loud + ly ______________

Directions: Add the suffix *-ly* and write the new word.

Home Activity: Have your child use each word in a sentence.

Name ______________________________

Circle and write.

1. 
coat

2. 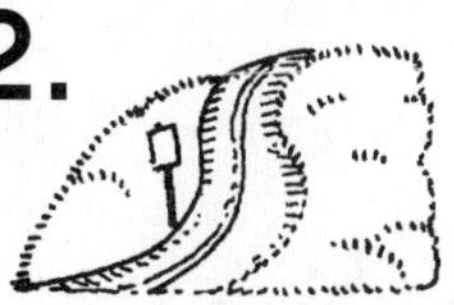
road

3. 
tow

4. 
roast

5. 
crow

Directions: In each row, circle the picture whose name rhymes with the word and write the picture name.

Home Activity: Help your child make a list of long *o* words with *oa* or *ow*.

Name ______________________________

Circle.

1.

sh tch

2.
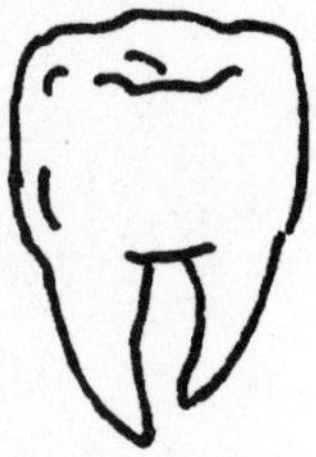

ch th

3.
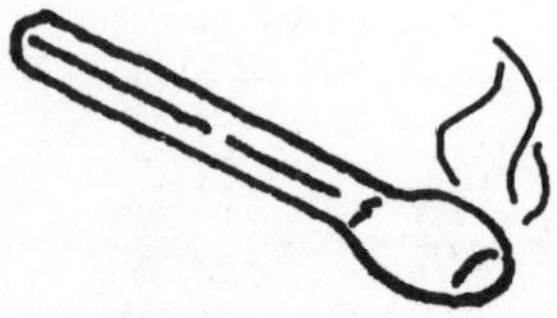

th tch

4.

sh ch

5.

sh th

6.

ch th

7.

sh ch

8.
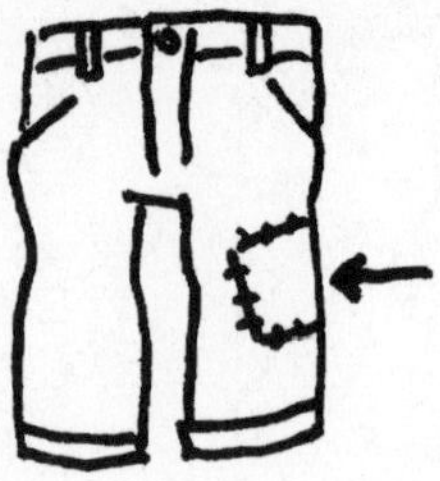

th tch

Directions: Circle the letters that stand for the ending sound in the picture name.

Home Activity: Help your child write the picture names in a list.

Name ______________________________

fork

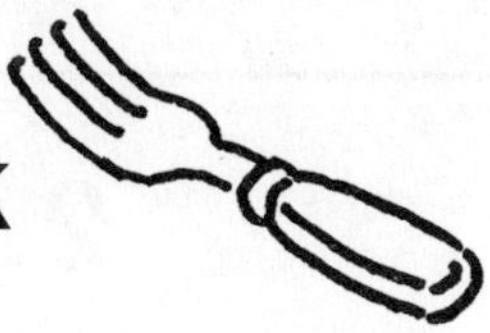

Color.

1. 

2. 

3. 

4. 

5. 

6. 

7. 

8. 

9. 

10. 

Directions: Color the picture if the picture name has the same vowel sound as *fork*.

Home Activity: Help your child write a story about a horse.

Name ____________________

Write.

1. 

h__ __n

2. 

f__ __t

3. 

st__ __k

4. 

h__ __se

5. 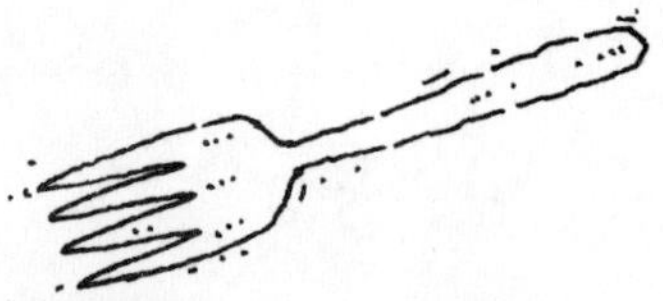

f__ __k

6. 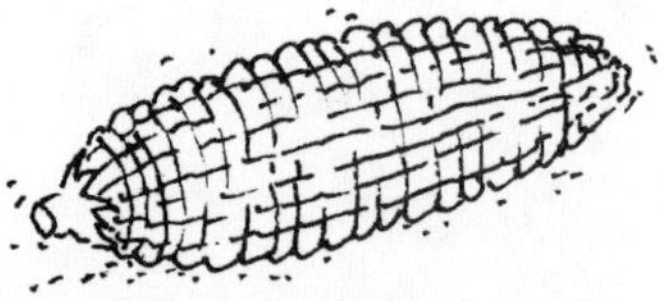

c__ __n

7. 

st__ __e

8. 

p__ __ch

Directions: Write the letters that finish each word.

Home Activity: Write *or* on paper. Help your child look for pictures that have *or* and paste them on the paper.

Name ______________________________

wave + ing = waving

Write.

1. like + s

2. bite + ing

3. rain + ed

4. go + es

5. bake + ing

6. stop + s

7. hike + ed

8. walk + s

Directions: Follow the signs to make a new word. Write the word.

Home Activity: Have your child add other endings to each word.

Name ______________________

Circle and write.

1.

jar
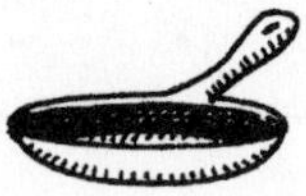

2.

park

3.
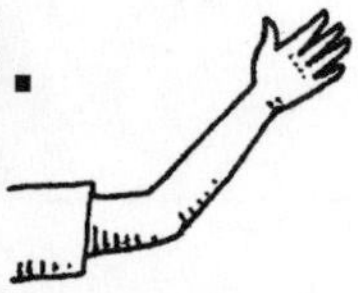
arm

4.

barn

5.
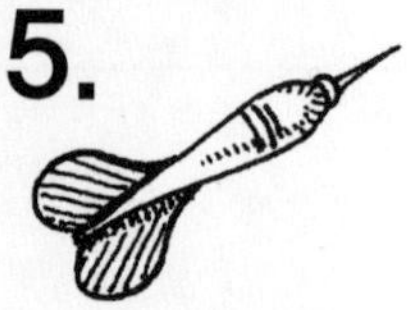
dart

Directions: Circle the picture whose name rhymes. Write the picture name. Underline the letters that spell the vowel sound.

Home Activity: Help your child write the other picture names.

Name ______________________________

Draw lines.

1.  popcorn

2.  sunshine

3. 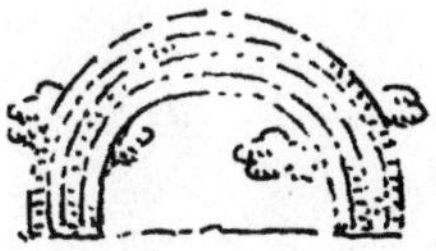 mailbox

4. 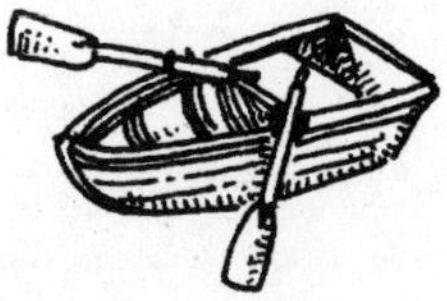 rainbow

5.  rowboat

6. 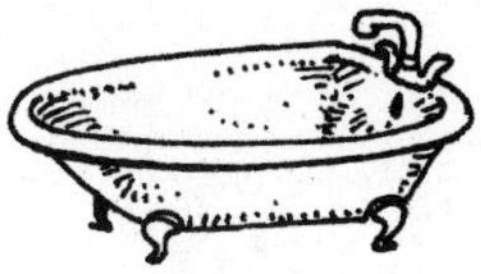 baseball

7.  bathtub

8.  raincoat

Directions: Draw lines to match the pictures with the words. Then draw a line to divide each compound word.

Home Activity: Help your child find other compound words to read and write.

Name ______________________________

bird 

Color.

1. 

2. 

3. 

4. 

5. 6

6. 30

7. 

8. 

9. 

10. 

Directions: Color the picture if the picture name has the same vowel sound as *bird.*

Home Activity: Read a story and have your child listen for words with the vowel sound in *bird.*

Name ______________________

Circle and write.

1.

door

dirt

2.

nose

nurse

3.

fern

fan

4.

game

girl

5.

bat

burn

6.

herd

hen

Directions: Circle and write the word that names the picture. Underline the letters that stand for the vowel sound.

Home Activity: Write *ir, er,* and *ur* on paper. Have your child write the picture names by the letters for the vowel sound.

Name ______________________

fast faster fastest

Write.

smaller smallest

1. This pet is the ______________ of all.

This pet is ______________ than mine.

higher highest

2. That hill is the ______________ of all.

This hill is ______________ than that one.

Directions: Write the best word to finish each sentence.

Home Activity: Ask your child to use *softer/softest* and *bigger/biggest* in sentences.

Name ______________________________

Circle and write.

1.
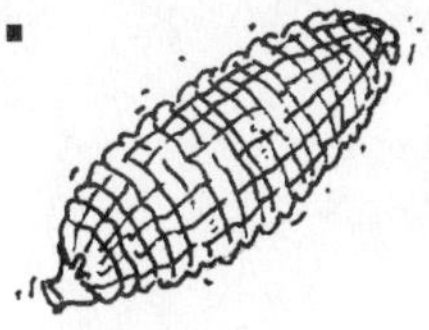
corn

2.

stork

3.

torch

4.

core

5.

sort

Directions: Circle the picture whose name rhymes. Write the picture name. Underline the letters that spell the vowel sound.

Home Activity: Help your child write rhyming words for *core: wore, tore, sore, more, shore, snore.*

Name ______________________

Write.

1. I am ______________ a cake.

   make + ing

2. She ______________ her friend.

   help + s

3. He ______________ a pet.

   want + ed

4. She ______________ the ball.

   catch + es

5. Teri is ______________ the bus.

   ride + ing

Directions: Add the ending and write the new word to complete the sentence.

Home Activity: Ask your child to add endings to these words: *smile, save, like, bake.*

Name ______________________

cow

Color.

1.

2.

3.

4.

5.

6.

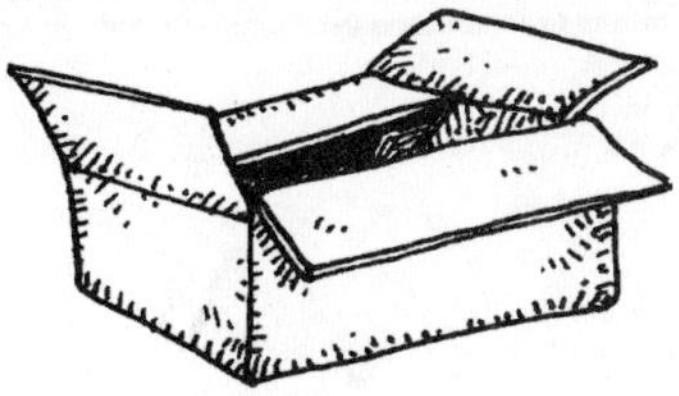

7.

8.

9.

10.

Directions: Color the picture if the picture name has the same vowel sound as *cow.*

Home Activity: Help your child make a list of words that have the vowel sound in *cow.*

Name ____________________

Write.

1. 

t__er

2. 

pl__

3. 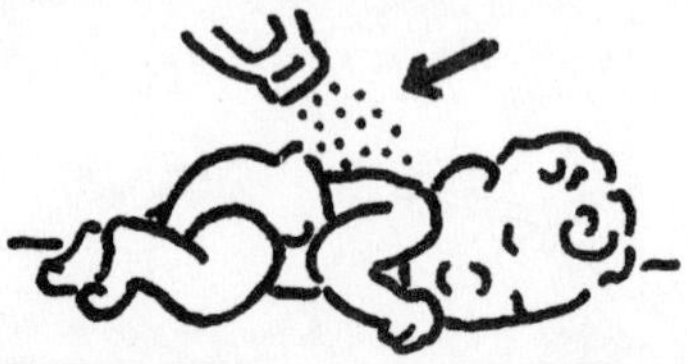

p__der

4. 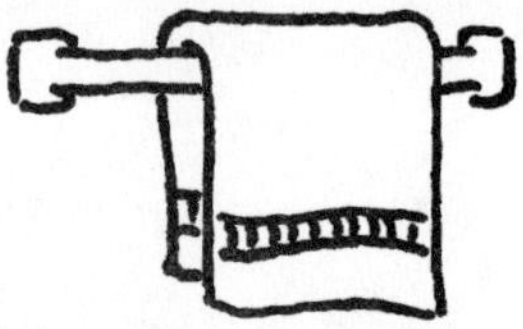

t__el

5. 

fl__er

6. 

cr__n

7. 

c__

8. 

fr__n

Directions: Write the letters that finish each word.

Home Activity: Point to a word and have your child use it in a sentence.

Name ______________________

Write.

1. ham	☐	2. hammer	☐
3. pen	☐	4. pencil	☐
5. cabin	☐	6. cab	☐
7. can	☐	8. candy	☐
9. win	☐	10. window	☐

Directions: Say each word. Write the number that tells how many parts each word has.

Home Activity: Help your child search for words with more than one word part.

Name ________________________

Circle and write.

1.

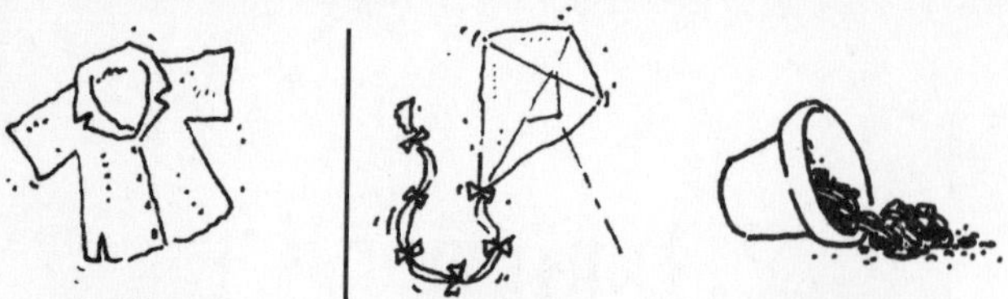

shirt | kite dirt

2.

bird | herd six

3.

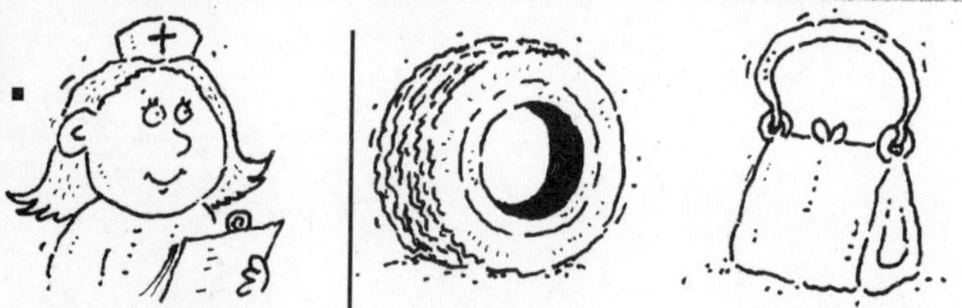

nurse | tire purse

4.

stir | mice fur

5.

turn | burn bike

Directions: Circle the picture whose name rhymes. Write the picture name. Underline the letters that spell the vowel sound.

Home Activity: Help your child make a list of *ir, er,* and *ur* words.

Name ______________________________

Draw lines.

1. a cow's bell

2. a cub's tree

3. a duck's foot

4. a fish's fin

5. a dog's bone

Directions: Draw lines to match the words to the pictures.

Home Activity: Help your child make possessives using your child's name—Tom's book, Tom's pet, Tom's pencil.

Name ______________________________

shout

Color.

1.

2.

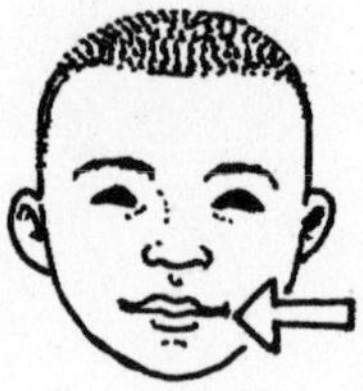

3.

4.

5.

6.

7.

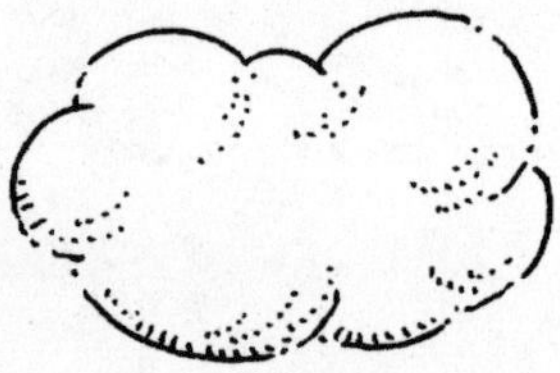

8.

9.

10.

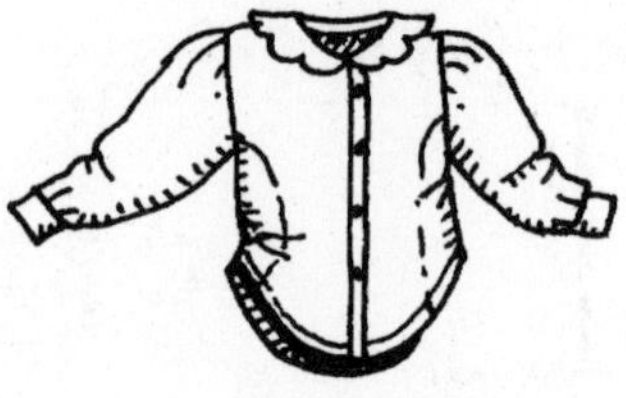

Directions: Color the picture if the picture name has the same vowel sound as *shout.*

Home Activity: Help your child make a list of *ou* words.

Name ______________________________

Write.

1. 

h _ _ se

2. 

cl _ _ d

3. 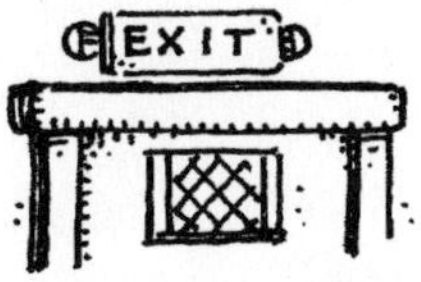

_ _ t

4. 

c _ _ nt

5.  

sh _ _ t

6. 

m _ _ se

7. 

bl _ _ se

8. 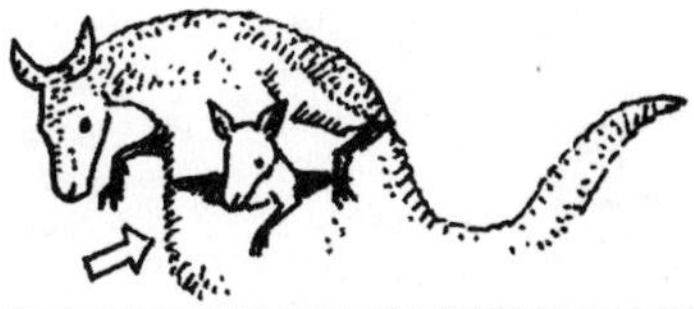

p _ _ ch

Directions: Write the letters that finish each word.

Home Activity: Make word puzzles and have your child find the *ou* word: *m o u* ***m o u s e*** *b o u n.*

Name ______________________

bacon  hammer 

Draw lines.

1.

rabbit 

ball 

tiger 

2.

pen 

penny 

cabin 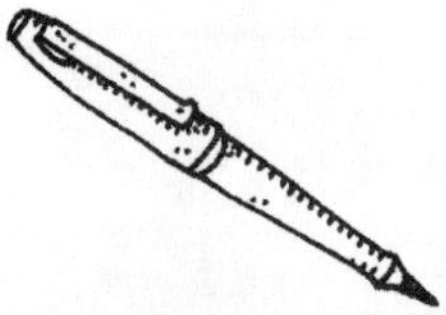

3.

pilot 

car 

carrot 

4.

mitten 

block 

medal 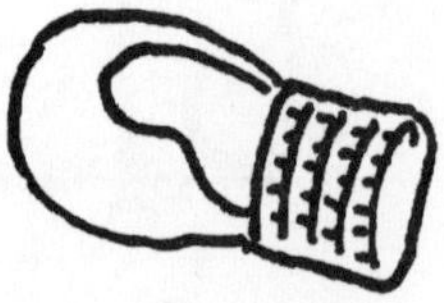

Directions: Draw lines to match the words with the pictures. Underline the letter(s) that stand for middle consonant sounds.

Home Activity: Point to a word and have your child use the word in a sentence.

Name ______________________________

Circle and write.

1.

clue

cube

glue

2.

flew

blew

tree

3.

true

blue

mule

4.

stew

jeep

crew

5.

threw

wheel

chew

Directions: Circle the picture whose name rhymes. Write the picture name. Underline the letters that spell the vowel sound.

Home Activity: Point to and read a word. Have your child name the letters that stand for the vowel sound.

Name ______________________________

more than fast = faster

most fast = fastest

Write.

1. more than tall

2. most tall

3. more than slow

4. most slow

5. more than old

6. most old

7. more than low

8. most low

Directions: Write the *-er* or *-est* word that answers each clue.

Home Activity: Help your child create sentences using the *-er* and *-est* words on the page.

Name ______________________

boy  boil 

Circle and write.

1. 

coin

coil

2. 

spoil

soil

3. 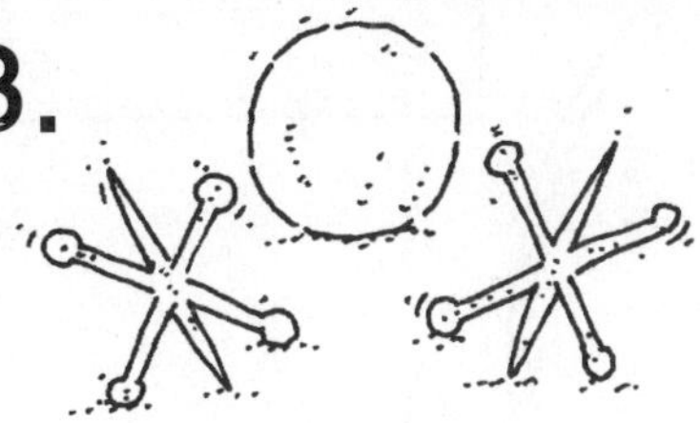

toil

toy

4. 

foil

broil

5. 

point

joy

6. 

enjoy

cowboy

Directions: Circle and write the word that names the picture. Color the picture.

Home Activity: Help your child read the words and tell what letters stand for the vowel sound.

Name ______________________________

Write and circle.

Across

3. works on a ranch
5. a name for dirt

Down

1. something to play with
2. kind of money
4. way to cook meat

Words
broil
coin
toy
cowboy
soil

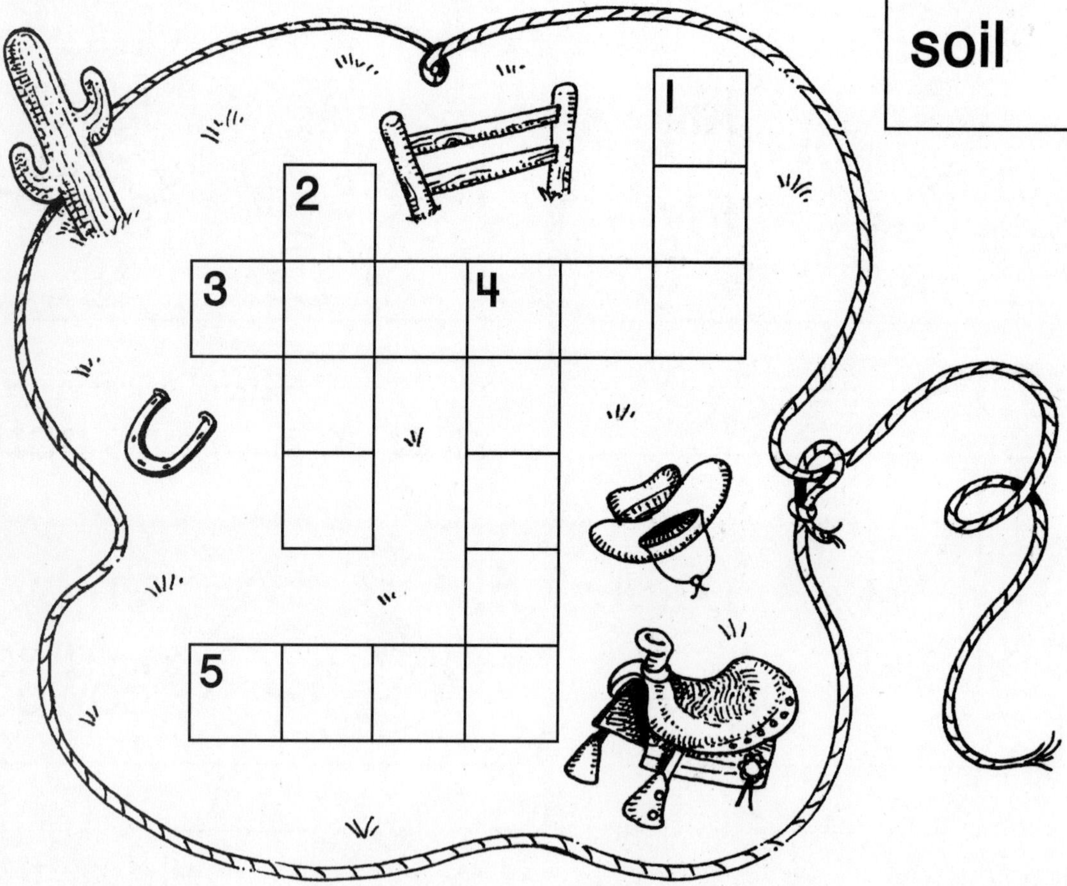

Directions: Write words to finish the puzzle. Circle *oi* or *oy* in each word in the list.

Home Activity: Help your child use *oi* and *oy* words to build a puzzle.

Name ______________________

ham 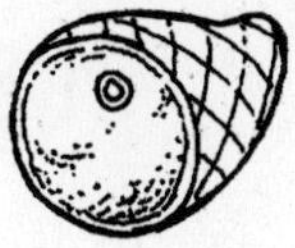

hammer 

Draw lines.

1.

rain 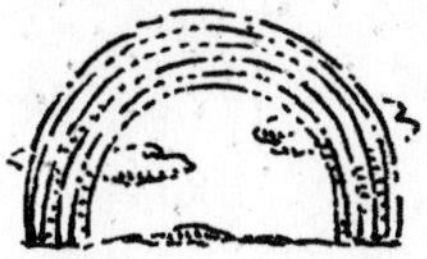

raincoat 

rainbow 

2.

running 

rides 

raked 

3.

sand 

sandpaper 

sandbox 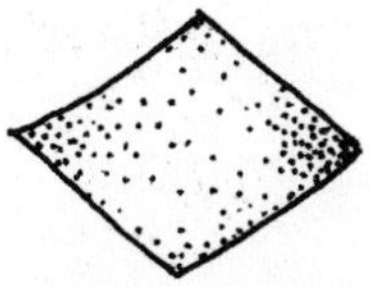

4.

couldn't	was not
didn't	could not
wasn't	did not

Directions: Draw lines to match the words with the pictures or words.

Home Activity: Point to a word and have your child read the word.

Name ______________________

cow  cloud 

Circle and write.

1. 
toad
tower

2. 
house
horse

3. 
mouth
moon

4. 
flower
flag

5. 
monkey
mouse

6. 
crown
crowd

Directions: Circle and write the word that names the picture. Color the picture.

Home Activity: Help your child read each word and tell what letters stand for the vowel sound.

Name ______________________

Circle and write.

1. We walked ______________________ .

slow slowly

2. The deer ran ______________________ .

quick quickly

3. The sun shines ______________________ .

bright brightly

4. The pillow is ______________________ .

soft softly

Directions: Circle the word that correctly completes the sentence. Write the word.

Home Activity: Have your child add *-ly* to the following words and write the new words: *glad, warm, deep.*